Your DIY Guide to
Federal Tax Credit

REMODEL
REPLACE
REFUND!

Creative Publishing
international

MINNEAPOLIS, MINNESOTA
www.creativepub.com

**Creative Publishing
international**

Copyright © 2009
Creative Publishing international, Inc.
400 First Avenue North, Suite 300
Minneapolis, Minnesota 55401
1-800-328-0590
www.creativepub.com
All rights reserved

Printed at R.R. Donnelley

10 9 8 7 6 5 4 3 2 1

Library of Congress Cataloging-in-Publication Data

Remodel, replace, refund! : your DIY guide to the 2009-2010 federal tax
credit for homeowners / [created by the editors of Creative Publishing
international, Inc.].
    p. cm.
  Includes index.
  Summary: "Teaches homeowners how to earn up to $1,500 in direct tax
credits by showing how to take advantage of the energy incentives in the
Federal Stimulus Plan and doing their own remodeling"--Provided by
publisher.
  ISBN-13: 978-1-58923-514-4 (soft cover)
  ISBN-10: 1-58923-514-2 (soft cover)
  1. Dwellings--Maintenance and repair--Amateurs' manuals. 2. Energy
tax credits--United States. I. Creative Publishing International. II.
Title: Your DIY guide to the 2009-2010 federal tax credit for homeowners.

  TH4817.3.R44 2009
  644--dc22

2009028982

President/CEO: Ken Fund
VP for Sales & Marketing: Kevin Hamric

Home Improvement Group

Publisher: Bryan Trandem
Managing Editor: Tracy Stanley
Senior Editor: Mark Johanson
Editor: Jennifer Gehlhar

Creative Director: Michele Lanci-Altomare
Senior Design Managers: Jon Simpson, Brad Springer
Design Manager: James Kegley

Lead Photographer: Joel Schnell
Shop Manager: James Parmeter

Production Managers: Laura Hokkanen, Linda Halls

Page Layout Artist: Tina R. Johnson
Shop Help: Charlie Boldt
Contributing Author & Editor: Eric Smith

Remodel, Replace...Refund!
Created by: The Editors of Creative Publishing international, Inc.

Contents

REMODEL
REPLACE
REFUND!

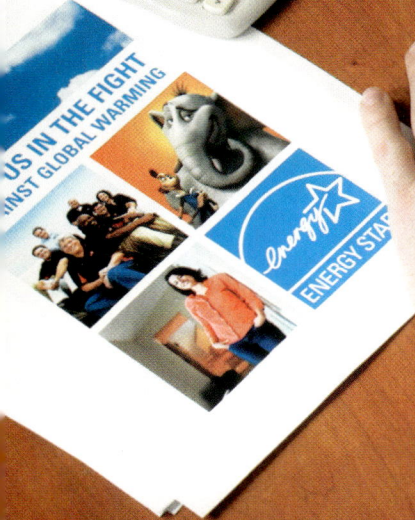

Introduction

If you're unhappy about high utility bills and want to do something about saving energy, there's never been a better time.

As part of the American Recovery and Reinvestment Act (The Stimulus Plan), the United States government has begun to put serious financial muscle behind energy conservation programs, encouraging homeowners to invest in energy efficiency by offering generous tax credits of up to $1,500 for qualifying home improvements in 2009 and 2010. We're not talking about ordinary tax deductions here, where the amount is subtracted from your gross income before taxes: these dollars come straight from the bottom line after you have calculated how much you owe or are owed. That's up to $1,500 you don't have to pay in taxes or $1,500 added directly to your refund.

The program covers a wide range of energy-saving products and improvements, including windows, entry doors, garage doors, insulation, furnaces, water heaters, and roofs. Almost any major project you do on your house that saves energy is eligible for a substantial credit as long as you use materials that meet the program guidelines. You can earn even more if you install energy-generating technology like solar panels or wind energy or geothermal heat pumps—30 percent of the total cost, with no upper limit, as long as you buy and install the system anytime from 2009 through 2016. This means that the $20,000 solar panel installation that just didn't quite make sense a few years ago is now a $14,000 system that could pay for itself years sooner.

Whether you're installing solar panels, replacing inefficient windows or insulating your attic, energy-saving improvements can pay big dividends: first, they lower your utility bills; second, they lessen pollution by decreasing the amount of coal or oil or gas that must be burned to create electricity; and third, they help strengthen the economy by keeping factories busy and encouraging investment in new and more efficient technologies.

In this book, we'll explain how the program works, what it covers, and how you can take advantage of it. Plus, we'll show you how to locate additional rebate and incentive programs from state governments and utility companies that can lower your costs even further. We'll explain how to evaluate your expenses and your energy use and estimate your potential savings. And finally, we'll show you step-by-step how you can do the work yourself—an especially important aspect, because credits for the most popular projects, such as replacing windows and doors, apply only to material costs and do not reimburse for labor.

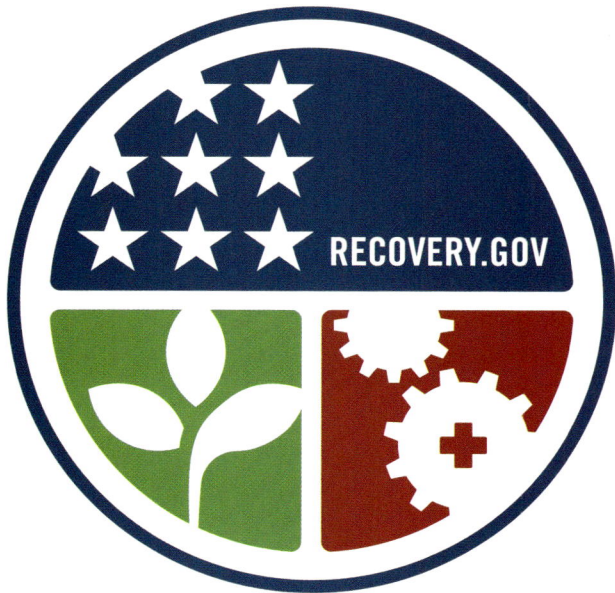

The American Recovery & Reinvestment Act (ARRA), better known as the Stimulus Plan, was unveiled in February 2009 to boost the U.S. economy. Among the most popular components are the energy tax credits for homeowners, which provide direct tax credits for qualifying improvements you make to your home.

THE PROGRAM & HOW IT WORKS

The federal tax credits for energy efficiency included in the Stimulus Plan have many goals. The primary objective is to subsidize the high initial costs of energy-saving products and renewable energy technology, so "green" solutions are competitive with cheaper (but less efficient) products and energy sources. It does this by allowing taxpayers to subtract a large part of the cost from their taxes as a credit. For example, if you buy $5,000 worth of qualifying windows, you can subtract 30 percent of that cost ($1,500) from your tax bill, even if you're already receiving a refund. Essentially the government is giving you a check for 30 percent of your cost, though you have to wait a few months and do a little paperwork to earn it. (And, this being the IRS, there are some caveats that we'll get to later.)

ARRA Tax Credits Timeline ▸

Jan. 1, 2009: Qualifying products bought after this date become eligible for a 30% tax credit.

Feb. 17, 2009: President Obama announces the Federal Tax Credits for Homeowners program as part of the American Recovery and Reinvestment Act (the "Stimulus Bill").

June 1, 2009: "Grandfather period" for window and door standards ends. From Jan. 1 to June 1, 2009, any window or door with an Energy Star label qualified for the tax credit. After June 1, windows and doors must have a U factor greater than or equal to .30 and an SHGC greater than or equal to .30.

Dec. 31, 2009: Eligibility deadline for 2009 tax year. Qualifying products must be placed in service by this date.

April 15, 2010: Taxes and documentation for 2009 tax year due. Fill out IRS Form 5695 and Form 1040. Keep receipts and Manufacturer Certification Statement for your records.

Dec. 31, 2010: Tax credit program ends for insulation, windows, doors, roofs, central heating and air conditioning, air source heat pumps, boilers, water heaters (except solar), and biomass stoves. The program continues for geothermal heat pumps, solar hot water heaters, solar panels, small wind turbines, and fuel cells.

April 15, 2011: Taxes and documentation for 2010 tax year due. Fill out IRS Form 5695 and Form 1040.

Dec. 31, 2016: Tax credit program ends for geothermal heat pumps, solar hot water heaters, solar panels, small wind turbines, and fuel cells.

April 15, 2017: Taxes and documentation for 2016 tax year due. Fill out IRS Form 5695 and Form 1040.

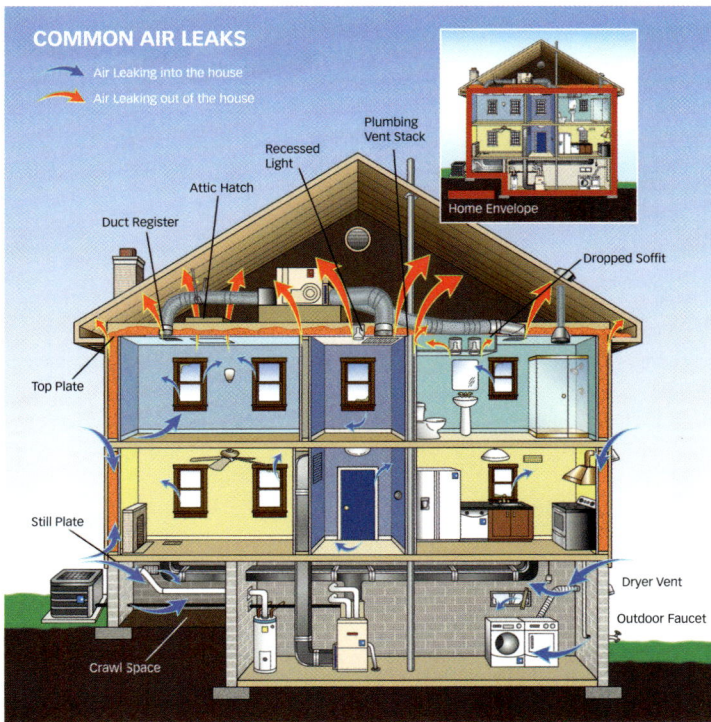

COMMON AIR LEAKS

→ Air Leaking into the house
→ Air Leaking out of the house

Plumbing Vent Stack
Recessed Light
Attic Hatch
Duct Register
Top Plate
Still Plate
Crawl Space
Home Envelope
Dropped Soffit
Dryer Vent
Outdoor Faucet

Buy energy saving products and save 30% on almost any project in your house that either reduces energy consumption or generates energy from renewable sources.

The energy conservation part of the tax credit program helps pay for remodeling and replacement projects placed in service in 2009 and 2010 in existing houses only—30 percent of the cost up to $1,500 (for all improvements combined). For instance, replacement windows for the old part of your house and new windows for an addition both qualify, but windows for a new house do not qualify (new construction is covered by other government programs). This rule applies to tax credits for windows and doors, insulation, roofs, heating and air conditioning products, water heaters, and biomass stoves (stoves that burn wood, plant waste, pellets, or other renewable material).

If you're replacing or installing windows, doors, a roof, or insulation, the tax credit is based on the cost of the eligible products only, not the labor or other associated costs like lumber or siding. For central heating and air conditioning, water heaters, and biomass stoves the credit is based on both the eligible products and the labor (assuming you hire a contractor to do it), including labor involved in preparing the site—for example, removing old fixtures and pipes, roughing in new framing and plumbing, and other work associated with installation of the product.

The part of the program meant to encourage the development of renewable energy has different guidelines and more generous tax credits, since the initial costs can be considerably higher. Geothermal heat pumps, solar panels, solar hot water heaters, and small wind energy systems qualify whether they're used in existing homes, new homes, vacation homes, or rental property. Fuel cells also qualify, but only for a primary residence. Unlike energy conservation products, tax credits for renewable energy products are available for 2009 through 2016, are 30 percent of the entire cost—both labor and material— and can be spread over more than one tax year. So, if you install a wind energy system costing $30,000 for labor and materials, you'll get a tax credit of $9,000.

Q – Can tax credits be used for qualifying products in new houses?

A – The credits for energy conservation products like windows or furnaces can only be used for owner-occupied existing houses. Energy generating products like solar panels or geothermal heat pumps earn tax credits whether they're installed in new or existing houses, vacation houses, or rentals. Heat pumps qualify in owner-occupied new or existing houses only.

Q – Is the tax credit deducted from my total tax, including social security withholding?

A – No, just federal tax.

Q – Can I install new windows and solar panels and get tax credits for both?

A – Yes. There's no cap on the tax credit for solar panels and therefore no reason you can't get the credit for both. Remember that the credit for windows is only good for the year you put them in service (2009 or 2010), but the credit for solar panels can be carried forward to later years.

Q – Can I use the 1040 EZ form when I file?

A – No, you have to use the standard 1040 along with Form 5695.

Q – How long does it take to get the tax credit?

A – You can get it as soon as you file your tax return.

Q – I usually get a refund. Do I still qualify for the tax credit?

A – Yes, as long as the taxes you paid during the year are equal to or more than the total credits you claim.

Q – I don't pay anything for taxes because I have lots of tax credits for child care and education. Can I still take the energy efficiency tax credits?

A – Not if your tax credits already add up to more than the federal tax you paid.

Q – How do I find a furnace that qualifies for the tax credit?

A – The supplier will usually have labeled it already. Otherwise, check the criteria noted in this book or at energystar.gov against the specifications of the model you're looking at, or go to the manufacturer's web site.

Q – What is Energy Star?

A – A program established by the Department of Energy and the Environmental Protection Agency to promote energy-efficient products and practices.

Q – Do Energy Star products always qualify for the tax credit?

A – No, not always. Check the requirements in this book or at energystar.gov.

Quick Guide to Tax Credits ▸

Product	Maximum tax credit
For existing homes	
Windows, skylights, entry doors and garage doors	30% of product cost, $1,500 max.
Insulation	30% of product cost, $1,500 max.
Roofs (metal, asphalt, roll)	30% of product cost, $1,500 max.
Forced air furnace, boiler, central air, or heat pump	30% of product + labor cost, $1,500 max.
Water heater	30% of product + labor cost, $1,500 max.
Biomass stove	30% of product + labor cost, $1,500 max.
For new or existing homes, 2nd homes, or rentals	
Geothermal heat pump	30% of product + labor cost
Solar panels	30% of product + labor cost
Solar water heaters	30% of product + labor cost
Small wind energy systems	30% of product + labor cost
For new or existing houses	
Fuel Cells	30% of product + labor cost

Eligible Products & Projects

The tax credits are meant to save as much energy as possible and to encourage state-of-the-art technologies, which means that only the most energy-efficient products are covered. Each type of product has different criteria, and not all products that have earned Energy Star labels qualify for the tax credit. However, manufacturers and suppliers are all aware of the tax credit program and have lists of qualified products.

Before you start your project, either check with the manufacturer (or supplier) to find out which of their products qualify or consult the energystar.gov website, which has detailed requirements for each type of product along with links to manufacturers. Manufacturers must also have a "Manufacturer Certification Statement" for any qualifying product, and you'll need a copy of this for your taxes. Energy Star doesn't rate products for quality, so check with the Better Business Bureau, consumer magazines, internet sources, and installers and compare manufacturer warranties before you buy.

Quick Guide to Eligible Products ▸

Product	Qualifying specifications
Windows, skylights, entry doors	Before 6/1/09—Energy Star label After 6/1/09—SHGC and U factor < = 30%
Garage doors	SHGC and U factor < = .30 (garage must be insulated)
Storm doors and windows	U factor < = .30 in combination with door or window (check with manufacturer)
Insulation	Any type
Roofs (metal, asphalt, roll, coated)	Consult manufacturer or energystar.gov
Central air conditioner	Split systems: EER > = 13, SEER > = 16 Package systems: EER > = 12, SEER > = 14
Air source heat pump	Split systems: HSPF > = 8.5, EER > = 12.5, SEER > = 15 Package systems: HSPF > = 8, EER > = 12, SEER > = 14
Natural gas or propane furnace	AFUE > = 95
Oil furnace	AFUE > = 90
Gas, propane, or oil hot water boiler	AFUE > = 90
Gas, propane, or oil water heater	Energy factor > = .82 or thermal efficiency > = 90%. All gas tankless heaters with Energy Star label qualify
Electric heat pump water heater	Energy Star label
Biomass stove	Thermal efficiency > = 75%
Geothermal heat pump	Energy Star label
Solar panels	Energy Star label
Solar water heaters	Energy Star label
Small wind energy systems	Less than 100 kW capacity
Fuel cells	At least 30% efficiency and 0.5 kW capacity

Note: Some of these specifications are still preliminary. Check with the manufacturer or energystar.gov before purchasing.

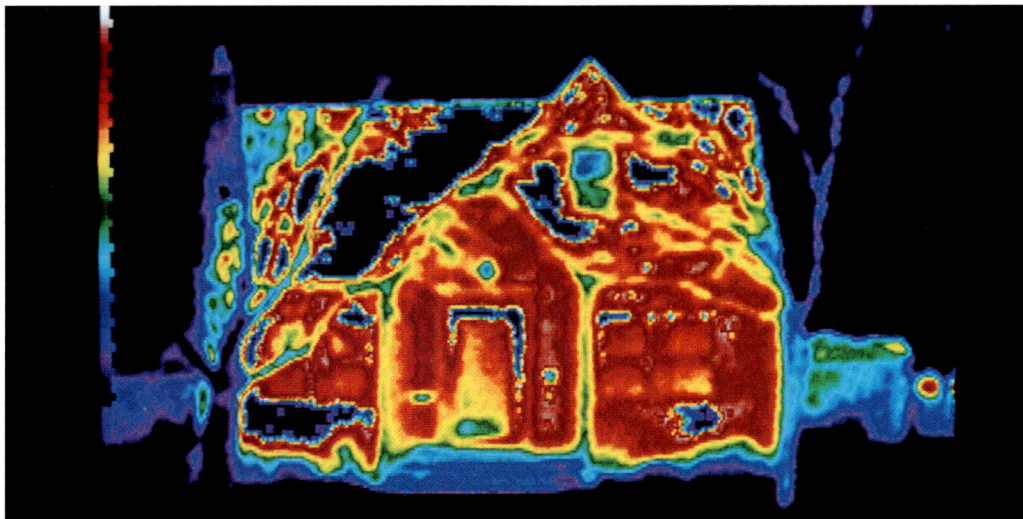

A thorough energy audit will identify the areas of your house that can benefit most from improvements, be they windows, doors, insulation, or HVAC upgrades. An infrared photo taken on a normal heating or cooling day will shed light on the subject. Check with your local utility company to get referrals for infrared photographers.

Choosing a Project

Unless you have enough money to do all your energy savings projects right away, you're probably going to need to prioritize—start with the project that will have the largest immediate benefit. In a well-insulated new house, this might be solar panels or a geothermal heat pump, but in an older house the biggest energy savings usually comes from adding more insulation or replacing drafty windows.

Start by inspecting your house for obvious problems. Look in the attic and in crawlspaces for missing or inadequate insulation. Heat rises; so, if you only have a few inches of ancient insulation in the attic, you're losing a lot of energy. Gaps under doors and around windows, open dryer vents, and uninsulated ducts can also waste a large amount of energy.

The next step is to look for hidden problems. You can find some of these yourself with an inexpensive infrared thermometer that measures surface temperatures with a beam of light, which can help you zero in on spots in your house that need more insulation or caulking. For a more thorough, whole house energy audit, you may want to hire an energy auditor. Many local utility companies also offer free or low cost audits.

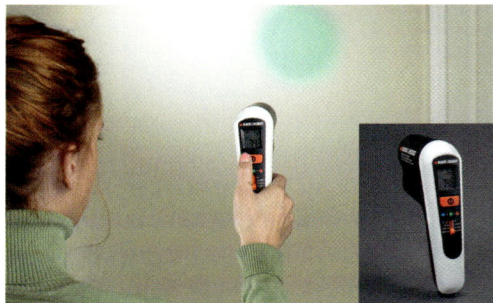

Pinpoint temperature differences in walls and ceilings due to gaps in the insulation by using an inexpensive remote-sensing thermometer.

Free DIY Air Leak Test ▸

Close all the doors and windows, then turn on all the exhaust fans. Hold a candle or a smoky stick of incense near outlets, baseboards, and around doors and windows to check for hidden drafts.

The Good Kind of Audit

If the word *audit* conjures a frightening image of a dour, gray-suited official from the IRS knocking at your door, don't worry; an energy audit is quite a different thing. Energy auditors are trained professionals who use special equipment and techniques to assess the energy performance of a home. In essence, they tell you where your energy dollars are going and offer suggestions for changes to lower your consumption and trim monthly utility bills.

Speaking of utility bills, your energy auditor will probably ask to see a year's worth of them, to look for usage patterns and possible aberrations that indicate system problems or, more likely, energy-wasting habits. But perhaps the most valuable service provided by energy auditors is in finding out where your house is leaking air and where it needs more insulation. To do this, auditors use a blower door and may use an infrared camera. A blower door seals over an exterior

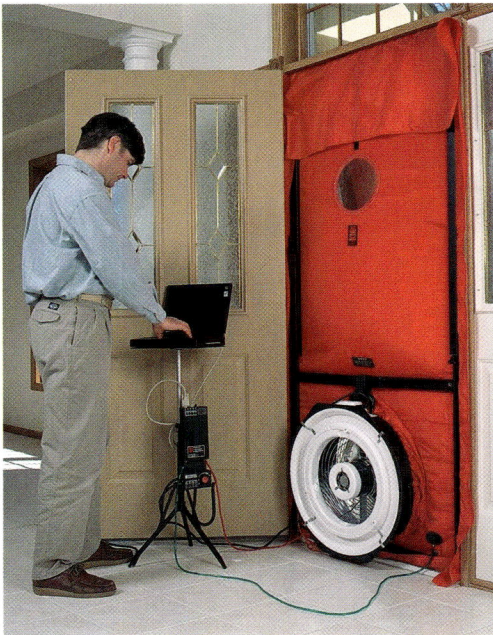

Energy auditors use blower doors and other specialized equipment to find where homes are leaking air and where they can benefit most from added insulation and other energy improvements.

door opening and has a fan that blows out, creating negative pressure (like a vacuum) inside the house. With the system running, an auditor uses monitoring equipment to pinpoint the major air leaks throughout the house.

An infrared camera, or thermo imaging, tells an auditor where heat is escaping through the walls and other surfaces of a house. For example, if your home's builder neglected to insulate the walls behind your kitchen cabinets (a bizarre yet all-too-common occurrence), it will show up as a dark area on the infrared image. Thermo imaging can also reveal places where insulation was installed improperly or where it has settled over the years, leaving gaps and uninsulated spaces in framing cavities.

In addition to visual and instrument tests on the thermal envelope, an auditor will check your heating and cooling systems for proper operation, temperature settings, potential air leaks, etc. Hot water heaters, major household appliances, and lighting are also considered for their role in the overall energy picture.

After the assessment, your energy auditor can recommend ways for getting the most energy bang for your improvement buck. An experienced auditor can also tell you what's appropriate for your house and the local climate, such as the right types of insulation to use and what you might do to seal or insulate a basement or crawlspace.

If you're planning to invest significant amounts of time and money into energy improvements, an energy audit is essential. You don't want to spend $15,000 to replace your old, leaky windows, when you could save just as much energy by adding $500 worth of insulation to your attic. Or you might want to do both, to double your energy savings. Even if your improvement plans are modest, an energy audit can quickly pay for itself with the knowledge you gain about your house and your living habits.

To find a qualified energy auditor, check with your state energy office and your utility company. They may employ auditors or can direct you to resources for finding them. Some community and municipal energy and conservation programs offer low-cost or subsidized energy audit services. You can also look in the phone book under Energy Management & Conservation Consultants.

Estimating Savings

Inspections and energy audits can help you understand which projects will save the most energy, but it's also a good idea to take a hard-nosed look at costs and savings from the work you want to do. Fortunately, you don't have to be an accountant to do this. Although every home is different, government and local utilities provide information and tools that make it easy to estimate how much you'll save in utility bills when you increase the energy efficiency in your house.

The basic calculation is the same whether you're putting in windows, replacing a water heater, or installing solar panels.

Cost/Benefit Example 1 ▸

Compare a tankless whole-house water heater with a conventional storage tank water heater that has a twelve year warranty. The energy use figures can be found at energystar.gov or on the water heaters.

Model	Cost	Annual cost x 12 years	Lifetime cost
Tankless	1,000 – 30% credit = 700	260 x 12 = 3,120	$3,820
Conventional	500	380 x 12 = 4,560	$5,060

The cost for the conventional heater may actually be quite a bit more than shown here, because most tankless heaters have a twenty year warranty.

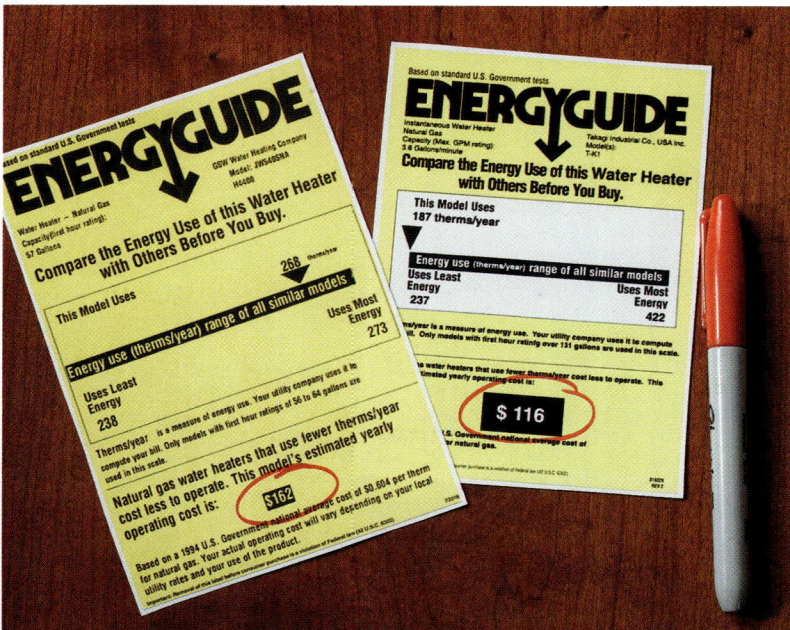

Energy-efficient products often have a higher initial cost than conventional products, but after you subtract the tax credit and compare the energy savings over the lifetime of the product, costs are often quite a bit less.

Cost/Benefit Example 2 ▸

Here's a more complicated scenario. The owner of an older house is trying to decide whether to spend $25,000 to insulate the whole house, replace an old furnace, and replace all the old single-pane windows. Energy costs and estimated savings are available from several sources: local utility companies can usually provide rough estimates of savings from various upgrades; if those aren't adequate, you can get highly detailed estimates of energy use customized to your house and area at either hes.lbl.gov (a government-sponsored website developed by the Lawrence Berkeley National Laboratory) or ase.org/content/article/detail/971 (The Alliance to Save Energy).

Project	Cost	Annual energy cost x 20 years	Lifetime cost
Remodel	25,000-1500 = 23,500	1900 x 20= 38,000	$61,500
Do nothing	0	3900 x 20= 78,000	$78,000

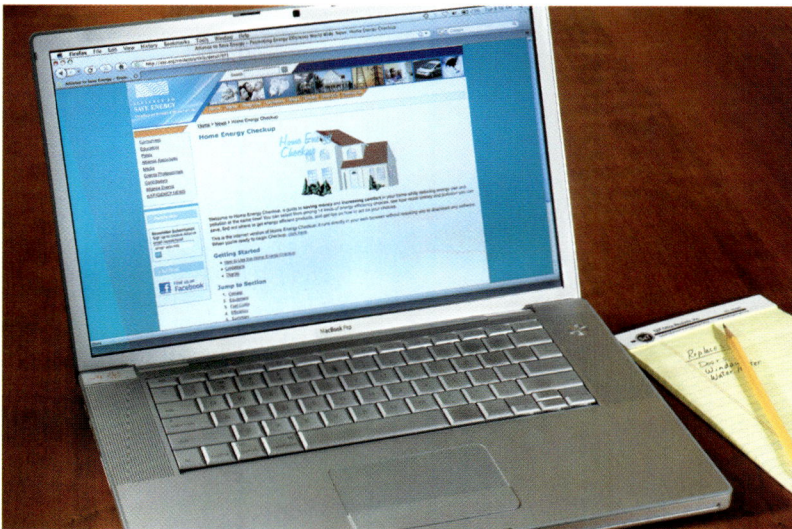

Use online resources to help you accurately evaluate the economic feasibility of various energy-savings projects you are considering for your home. See page 91 for a list of resources.

Does Generating Your Own Electricity Pay? ▸

The short answer is—sometimes. Solar, wind, geothermal heat pumps, and fuel cells are all exciting, rapidly evolving technologies and getting a credit for 30% of the total cost makes a huge difference, but the upfront costs are still high and prices and savings are heavily dependent on local weather conditions, Energy Star, and state and local rebates. For instance, solar pays for itself fairly quickly in the cloudless southwest, but takes much longer in the cloudy, rainy northwest. And wind power only pays off if you have lots of wind year round.

Before you invest in an electrical generating system, make your house as energy efficient as possible so that you're not wasting the energy you create. After that, get prices from local suppliers or installers, subtract the 30% tax credit and any local rebates, and then compare the costs and savings over the course of the system's lifetime to the cost of simply paying your monthly bill. Remember, the tax credits for energy generating equipment are good through 2016. Solar panels might be a little too expensive today, but a great deal tomorrow.

The Paperwork

The tax credits can be used to reduce the price (including sales tax) of qualifying products bought from January 1, 2009 to December 31, 2010—or through 2016 for energy generating improvements. Unlike a deduction, the total tax credit is subtracted directly from your taxes, reducing what you owe or increasing your refund. There is no income limitation for the tax credit.

Save a copy of the sales receipt and the "Manufacturer Certification Statement," which certifies that the product meets energy efficiency requirements. You don't need to send these with your return, but hold on to them in case you get audited. Certification statements can be printed from the manufacturer's website or will come with the product. Consult energystar.gov (look for the Tax Credits link at bottom left) before you buy anything to make sure the product and tax guidelines haven't changed. You can submit questions to Energy Star by phone or email through the "Contact Us" link.

IRS Red Flags ▸

Your total tax credits (lines 47 to 54) can't be higher than the tax you paid (not including Social Security and Medicare payments) in the year you claim the credit. If your tax on line 46 of Form 1040 is only $1,000, then the maximum credit you can claim for that year is only $1,000, not $1,500. However, the large credits from energy-generating products like solar panels can be spread over several tax years.

If you're married, filing jointly, you get only one $1,500 credit. If you're married, filing separately, you can each claim a $1,500 credit.

You can use part of the credit in 2009 and the rest in 2010 for a different project, but the total credit for those two years can't exceed $1,500 for all projects—unless you're doing a project like solar panels that has no cap.

You can't add labor to the cost unless it's specifically allowed (see page 8).

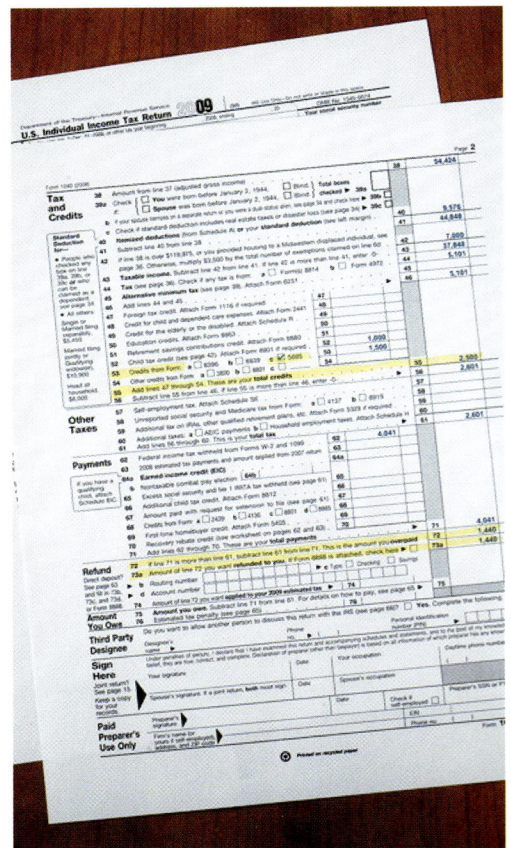

Claim the credit when you file your tax return. Fill out Form 5695 (available in late 2009), and then enter the total in Line 53 of Form 1040, where it will be subtracted from your taxes.

State & Local Incentives

Federal tax credits aren't the only way to save money on energy-efficient products. Many state and local governments and local utility companies encourage energy conservation with low-interest loans, grants, and rebates that can substantially reduce your costs. And remember, if you install wind or solar power and create more power than you consume, your meter will run backwards, resulting in credits or payments from the utility company.

You can locate these programs through several different sources. The first place to check is your local utility company. Almost all utility companies promote conservation because it's a cheaper and easier way to meet power demand than building new power plants. Thus, offering a rebate of several hundred dollars for a tankless water heater or high-efficiency heat pump (as many utilities do) ultimately can save the utility company as much money as it does the customer.

Some state and local governments also employ officials specifically to deal with energy issues. They can give you up-to-date information on incentives. You can find email addresses and phone numbers at naseo.org (National Association of State Energy Officials), or simply call the information phone number for your state government (see page 92).

The Database of State Incentives for Renewables & Efficiency (DSIRE) also maintains a directory of incentives in all fifty states at dsireusa.org—an easy way to window shop through all the programs in your area.

Find state and local government incentives, utility programs, and rebates as well as links to other relevant information by clicking on your state in the map of the United States on websites that manage this data (see Resources, page 91).

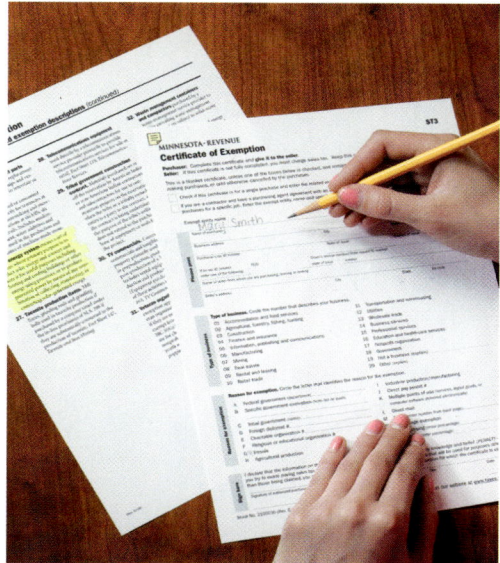

State and local programs that are independent from the ARRA plan have been in existence for some time and offer many useful opportunities.

Don't Waste Tax Credits ▸

Credits for energy conservation products (but not energy generating products) have to be used when they're put into service. If it looks like you'll have more tax credits than you can use, consider spreading your projects out over 2009 and 2010.

Upgrading windows can have a relatively fast payback in energy savings, even if your windows aren't particularly old or in bad condition. Passive solar heat gain from a new skylight or increased efficiency from a new exterior door or garage door can also qualify as program-eligible improvements.

WINDOWS, SKYLIGHTS, & DOORS

Need to replace or add a window or exterior door? The first question you should ask is "What's the U factor?" If you buy a window, entry door, skylight, or garage door with a U factor (rate of warmth or cold leaking out) and SHGC (rate of solar heat coming in) of 0.30 or less, it will cost 30 percent less than a similar product with a U factor and SHGC of 0.31 or more. This means you can now buy a great window or door (generally with a longer warranty) for the price of a lesser-quality one, plus you'll reduce your utility bill every month.

Not all Energy Star products meet the standards for the tax credit, but most major door, window, and garage door manufacturers have at least a few models that qualify, and most have a link to their qualifying products on their websites. (However, if you bought an Energy Star window, door, or skylight between January 1, 2009 and June 1, 2009, you can claim the full tax credit.) The National Fenestration Rating Council (NFRC) label on windows and doors lists the U factor and SHGC. You can also look up specific manufacturers at nfrc.org. Installation costs are not covered by the tax credit, but sales tax is.

Qualification

Windows: Wood, vinyl clad, or composite windows in double hung, casement, awning, or slider styles—both new and replacement—all qualify for the credit as long as they meet the U-factor standard. However, small differences like simulated divided lites or the type of glass can change the U factor and SHGC, even for the same window, so check the labels. If you're installing a window assembly—for instance a large picture window flanked by small casement windows—and only the picture window qualifies, you can still get a credit for that part as long as you get an itemized receipt.

Doors: The entire door and frame must be replaced to qualify for the tax credit, but most door types can qualify if they have a 0.30 or less U factor and SHGC, though you may have to search a bit. Check the values on all components of the door—if the sidelights qualify but the door doesn't, you can still get the tax credits for the sidelights.

Garage doors: Garage doors can qualify for the tax credit if they meet the criteria, but they must be installed in an insulated garage. This does not have to be an attached garage, as long as it's insulated. Tracks do not have to be replaced. The credit applies to the door only, not the installation labor or the garage door opener.

Skylights: Skylights with Energy Star stickers qualify for the credit until June 1, 2009. Requirements for the U factor and SHGC have not been fully established for skylights and roof windows after that date, but it's expected that at least some skylights will still qualify for the tax credits. Check with manufacturers or energystar.gov for the latest information before you buy a skylight.

Storm doors and windows: Check with manufacturers or energystar.gov before purchasing a storm window or door, as the rules for these have not yet been established. Storm windows will qualify for the credit if their U factor combined with a default U factor for an existing window or door meets the overall requirement for that climate zone, but these numbers are not yet available.

An efficient skylight that brings needed light to a dark room can qualify for the tax credit program, but be sure to discuss your plans with an energy consultant or your local inspector. In some cases, adding a skylight can result in a net loss of energy.

A new garage door qualifies for the tax credit if it meets efficiency standards and is installed in an insulated garage.

Replacing inefficient windows with new, energy-saving models not only provides payback on utility costs, it can make a great improvement in the appearance of your house.

Replacement Windows

Replacement window is a misleading term because it is often applied exclusively to replacement window sashes with separate plastic jamb liners that are retrofitted into the jambs in an existing window opening. However this type does not qualify for the tax credit. The only replacement windows that qualify are the "window insert" type that fit into the existing frame or new windows with nailing flange or brickmold that completely replaces the old window and trim.

For the purposes of the tax credit program, a replacement window is any window that is installed in an existing house. In most cases, the new window will fit into the opening left by the old window, but there are no limitations on where the window goes. The new window may be double-hung, casement, hopper, a fixed picture window, or just about any other style as long as it meets the minimum standards for qualification, including a maximum U factor of .30 (see pages 8 to 9).

Matching Windows ▶

If you're just adding a few windows, you'll get the best match if you buy the same brand as your existing windows. Look for a manufacturer's name in the corner of the glass, on the hardware, or along the edge of the window sash.

Replacement sash windows with separate jamb liners are custom-made to fit into an existing window opening once the old sashes are removed. They come with jamb liners and their own control mechanisms. Unfortunately, they do not qualify for the tax credit program.

Window inserts are the most widely available replacement windows, and the easiest to install. Use this type if the window frame is square and in good condition. You can install inserts without removing the window casing or any siding. A few manufacturers sell insert-style casement, awning, or slider windows that will fit inside existing frames. Unlike replacement sashes, window inserts are essentially complete window units with their own jambs.

Flanged windows are available in all styles. You must loosen or pull off the siding around windows to remove an old window like this or to install a new one. Use this type if the old frame is out of square or rotted or if you're replacing an existing flanged window. This type is comparable in price to inserts, but can be more time-consuming to install. After installing it, you can either install brick mold or other trim over the flange, nail J-channel over the flange for vinyl or metal siding, or just butt the siding against the window.

Brickmold windows are also available in all styles and are commonly used for wood-sided houses. Use this type if the old frame and trim need replacing or an insert isn't available. Consult the manufacturer if you're replacing a window with wide, flat casing—most offer various sizes as an option.

How to Prepare for a Replacement Window

Measure the height and width of the window opening at the edges and the centers, and then use the smallest of the three measurements. Be sure to measure from wood jamb to wood jamb, not from the window stop molding or parting stop or from a plastic jamb liner (if there is one). For the vertical measurement, measure from the inside edge of the sill. Order a window to fit these dimensions.

Pry off the window stop molding and remove the lower window sash. With the lower window out, drop the upper window as far as possible and then pry out the parting stop (both sides). Remove the upper sash. If the window is a newer type with plastic jamb liners, look for metal nailing clips holding the jamb liner and pry them out. Save the window stop molding for re-use.

Option: Cut the sash cords if the existing ones are old and double hung. These sash cords support metal counterweights that will fall down into the bottom of the window opening when the cords are cut. You do not need to retrieve the counterweights, but it's a good idea to stuff insulation batts into the sash weight openings if you can access them.

Prepare the jambs. Remove old nails in the wood jambs and repair any wood damage. Paint the jambs with a coat of wood primer for extra protection before the new window is installed.

How to Install a Replacement Window

1

Apply caulk to the outside (blind) stop in the window opening. Apply it only to the top and sides. Use a paintable caulk rated for windows and doors.

2

Put the head expander and sill angle in place, if your windows have them. Slip a strip of an insulation batt between the window and the head expander and slip the expander over the window. Do not use fasteners. Also attach the sill angle to the outside of the window.

3

Tilt the window into place. Try to get it close to the final position and avoid removing the window once you have pressed it against the stops so you don't disturb the caulk lines. Check to make sure the window is level and adjust with shims, as needed. Remove any sash stops or other trim that may be concealing the predrilled installation holes in the window frame.

4

Attach the window. Push the head expander up and attach it with small screws (provided) if pressure alone will not keep it in place. Fasten the window by driving screws through the screw holes in the jambs. Don't overtighten the screws. Make sure the window is square—loosen or tighten the screws if it's not. Also adjust the center of the jamb with the adjusting screws so that the sash and the jamb are consistently parallel.

5

Hold the stop molding against the jamb and nail it in place after spraying minimal–expanding foam behind the window jambs. Caulk around the exterior of the new window insert.

Insulated glass panels that are separated by sealed inert gas were a great advance in energy efficiency, but the earlier versions tended to etch, creating cloudy or discolored glass (inset). The new tax credit program offers a great opportunity to replace these units with newer windows that have solved the etching problem.

How to Replace a Complete Window Unit

Prepare to remove the old window. Begin by prying off brickmold or other exterior trim that frames the window opening and pins the window frame to the house. If your old window is installed with nailing flanges, pry them loose once you have removed the brickmold. For casement windows (shown) disconnect the window closing hardware and, with a helper, remove the framed glass panel.

Remove the old window frame. Pry out and remove the old window jambs and casing to expose the studs of the framed rough opening. Clear old nails and debris from the opening. Inspect the old framing members, and replace as needed.

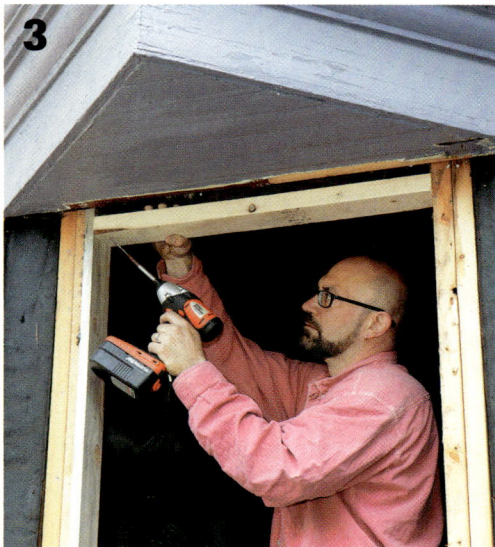

Add new framing members to the opening to reduce the size, if necessary. Here, a vertical 2 x 4 and 1 x 4 are added on top of the framed opening to reduce width by 2¼" to accommodate a slightly narrower window. A 2 x 4 header reduces the height. If you are replacing several windows in a wall make sure you keep the tops and bottoms aligned if you adjust the framing.

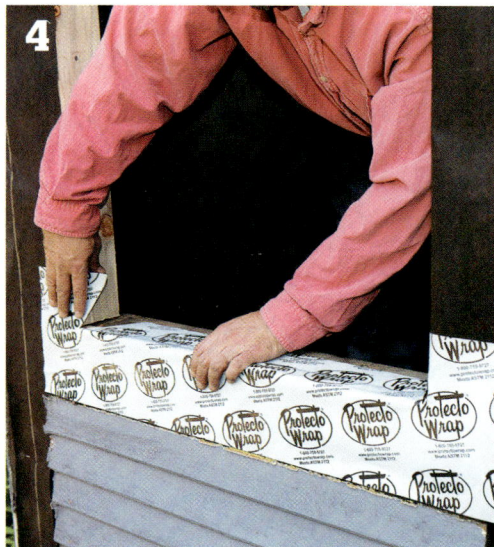

Prepare the opening for the new window. Test the fit of the new window and apply a strip of self-adhesive flashing to the windowsill (you can use builder's felt instead, but the flashing forms a better moisture barrier). The flashing should extend a few inches up the side jambs.

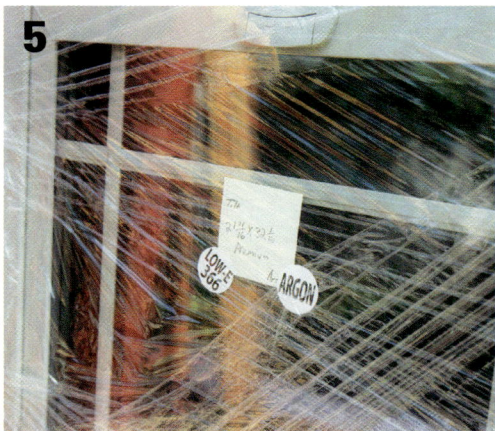

Unwrap the new window unit. Do not remove any identifying stickers until the after the window is installed and successful y inspected (if an inspection is required).

Set the new window unit into the opening. Place a few ¼"-thick shims on the sill first—there should be a slight gap beneath the window for caulk or sealant (unless your manufacturer's instructions suggest otherwise). Adjust the window so it is centered side to side.

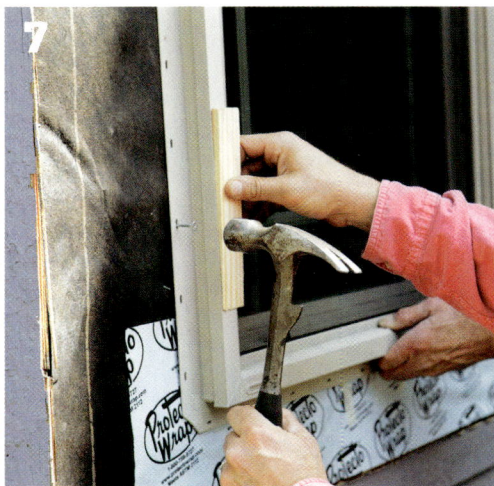

Tack the window in place by driving a 1½" roofing nail through a hole in a side nailing flange about 6" up from the bottom. With a helper stabilizing the window, hold a level on the top sash and pivot the window until it is level. Drive nails at the top corners to hold it in place. *TIP: Slip a shim between nail heads and the window frame to protect the frame from hammer damage.*

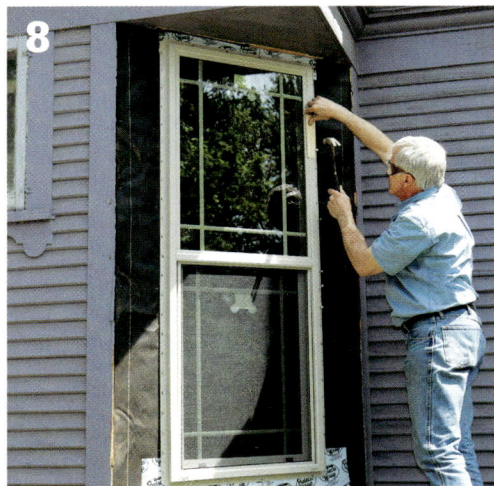

Complete the nailing schedule. Nailing flanges are predrilled with guide holes for nails at a specific spacing. Drive a roofing nail through each hole at the corners and every other hole at the sides.

Seal the window. Apply strips of self-adhesive flashing over the side nailing flanges and then over the top nailing flange, overlapping the strips by at least a couple of inches. If there is siding above the window top, insert drip-cap molding under the siding after the flashing is installed (inset). Use caulk to secure the drip cap—do not nail it.

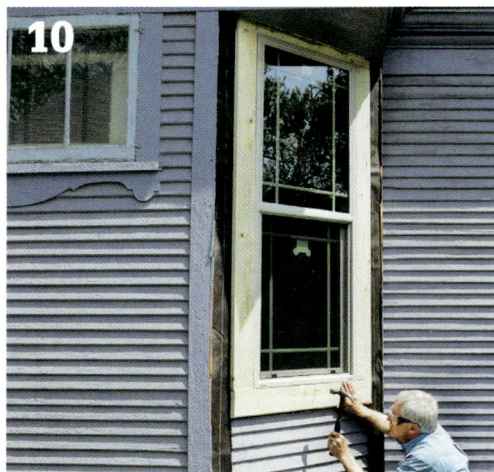

Trim around the window with casing or brickmold. Here, pieces of ⁵⁄₄ pine are cut to make bottom, side, and head casing. Apply a heavy bead of caulk to the back of each molding piece before installation and secure with 8d galvanized casing nails. Caulk gaps around the window and trim and then paint. Do not caulk between the bottom trim and bottom of the window. Seal and trim the interior side (see next page).

How to Finish the Interior

Fill uninsulated voids around window and door jambs with minimal expanding foam sealant or loosely packed insulation. Trim excess foam after it dries.

Place a length of casing along one side jamb, at a $1/8$" reveal. At the top and bottom of the molding, mark the points where horizontal and vertical reveal lines meet.

Drill pilot holes spaced every 12" to prevent splitting, and attach the vertical casings with 4d finish nails driven through the casings and into the jambs. Drive 6d finish nails into the framing members near the outside edge of the casings.

Measure the distance between the side casings, and cut top and bottom casings to fit, with ends mitered at 45°. If the window or door unit is not perfectly square, make test cuts on scrap pieces to find the correct angle of the joints. Drill pilot holes and attach with 4d and 6d finish nails.

Locknail the corner joints by drilling pilot holes and driving 4d finish nails through each corner, as shown. Drive all nail heads below the wood surface using a nail set, then fill the nail holes with wood putty.

New Windows

Add a window in an existing wall to introduce sunlight and increase passive solar heat gain.

Many windows must be custom-ordered several weeks in advance. To save time, you can complete the interior framing before the window unit arrives, but be sure you have the exact dimensions of the window unit before building the frame. Do not remove the outside wall surface until you have the window and accessories and are ready to install them.

Follow the manufacturer's specifications for rough opening size when framing for a window. The listed opening is usually one inch wider and one-half inch taller than the actual dimensions of the window unit. The following pages show techniques for wood-frame houses with platform framing.

If your house has masonry walls, you may want to attach your window using masonry clips instead of nails.

Recommended Header Sizes ▶

Rough Opening Width	Recommended Header Construction
Up to 3 ft.	$\frac{1}{2}$" plywood between two 2 × 4s
3 to 5 ft.	$\frac{1}{2}$" plywood between two 2 × 6s
5 to 7 ft.	$\frac{1}{2}$" plywood between two 2 × 8s
7 to 8 ft.	$\frac{1}{2}$" plywood between two 2 × 10s

Recommended header sizes shown above are suitable for projects where a full story and roof are located above the rough opening. This chart is intended for rough estimates only. For actual requirements, contact an architect or your local building inspector.

Insulated Headers ▶

For a 2 x 6 wall, assemble headers from three pieces of 2x wood with a piece of 1" thick rigid insulation sandwiched between two of the pieces. For a 2 x 4 wall, use ½" insulation instead of plywood.

New Lumber

Using an existing opening avoids the need for new framing. This is a good option in homes with masonry exteriors, which are difficult to alter. Order a replacement unit that is 1" narrower and $1/2$" shorter than the rough opening.

Enlarging an existing opening simplifies the framing. In many cases, you can use an existing king stud and jack stud to form one side of the new opening.

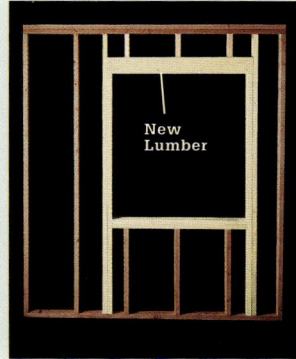

Framing a new opening is the only solution when you're installing a window or door where none existed or when you're replacing a unit with one that is much larger.

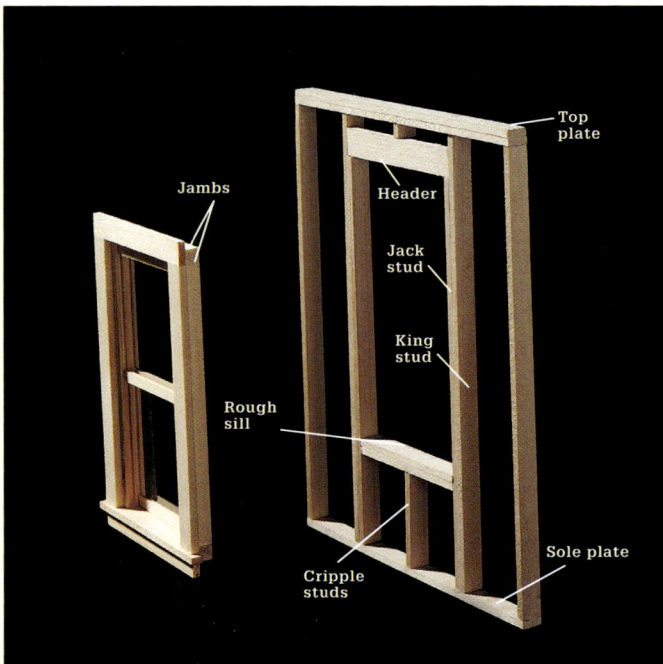

Jambs

Top plate

Header

Jack stud

King stud

Rough sill

Cripple studs

Sole plate

Window opening: The structural load above the window is carried by cripple studs resting on a header. The ends of the header are supported by jack studs and king studs, which transfer the load to the sole plate and the foundation of the house. The rough sill, which helps anchor the window unit but carries no structural weight, is supported by cripple studs. To provide room for adjustments during installation, the rough opening for a window should be 1" wider and $1/2$" taller than the window unit, including the jambs.

How to Frame a Window Opening

Measure and mark the rough opening width on the sole plate. Mark the locations of the jack studs and king studs on the sole plate. Where practical, use the existing studs as king studs.

Measure and cut the king studs to fit between the sole plate and the top plate. Position the king studs and toenail them to the sole plate with 10d nails.

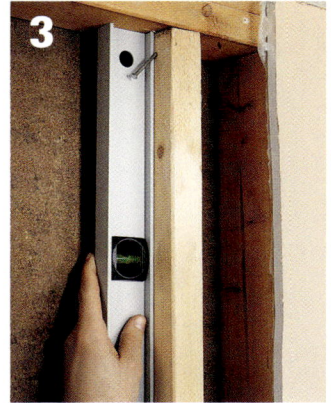

Check the king studs with a level to make sure they are plumb, then toenail them to the top plate with 10d nails.

Measuring from the floor, mark the top of the rough opening on one of the king studs. This line represents the bottom of the window header. For most windows, the recommended rough opening is $1/2$" taller than the height of the window frame.

Measure and mark where the top of the window header will fit against the king studs. The header size depends on the distance between the king studs. Use a carpenter's level to extend the lines across the old studs to the opposite king stud.

Measure down from the header line and mark the double rough sill on the king stud. Use a carpenter's level to extend the lines across the old studs to the opposite king stud. Make temporary supports if removing more than one stud.

7

Bottom
of sill

Set a circular saw to its maximum
blade depth, then cut through the
old studs along the lines marking the
bottom of the rough sill and along the
lines marking the top of the header. Do
not cut the king studs. On each stud,
make an additional cut 3" above the sill
cut. Finish the cuts with a handsaw.

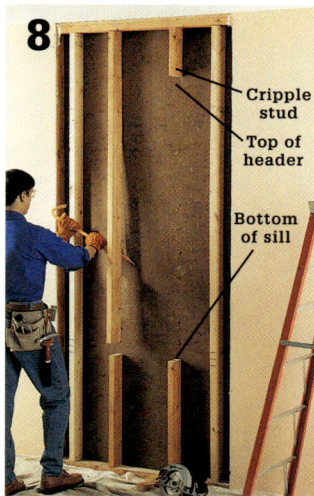

8

Cripple
stud

Top of
header

Bottom
of sill

Knock out the 3" stud sections, then
tear out the old studs inside the rough
opening using a pry bar. Clip away
any exposed nails using nippers. The
remaining sections of the cut studs will
serve as cripple studs for the window.

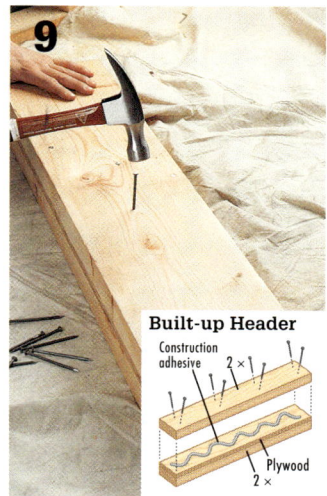

9

Built-up Header

Construction
adhesive   2 × 1

Plywood
2 ×

Build a header to fit between the king
studs on top of the jack studs, using
two pieces of 2× lumber sandwiched
around ½" plywood. Cut two jack studs
to reach from the top of the
sole plate to the bottom header lines
on the king studs.

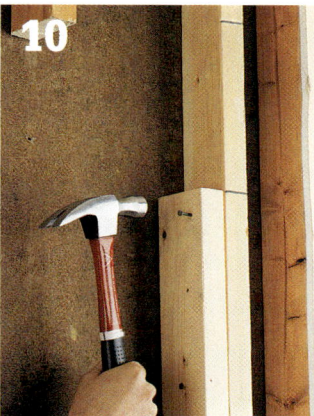

10

Nail the jack studs to the king studs
with 10d nails driven every 12". *Note:
On a balloon-framed house, the jack
studs will reach to the sill plate.*

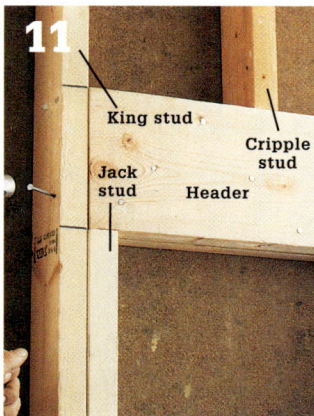

11

King stud

Cripple
stud

Jack
stud   Header

Position the header on the jack studs,
using a hammer if necessary. Attach the
header to the king studs, jack studs, and
cripple studs using 10d nails.

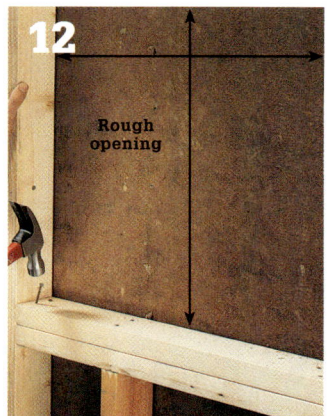

12

Rough
opening

Build the rough sill to reach between
the jack studs by nailing a pair of 2 × 4s
together. Position the rough sill on the
cripple studs, and nail it to the jack
studs and cripple studs with 10d nails.
Install window.

A skylight introduces natural light and a view of the sky, transforming dark or dull rooms. You can save 30 percent of the cost by purchasing one that meets the criteria for the tax credit.

Skylights

A fixed or operable skylight can qualify for the tax credit as long as it meets the criteria for U factor value and SHGC, even if it's a new installation (check at energystar.gov for updates on these criteria). A skylight provides welcome ventilation in the summer and extra light in the winter, and most models are not much more complicated to install than windows.

A skylight frame has a header and sill, similar to a standard window frame. However, instead of king studs it has king rafters as well as trimmers that define the sides of the rough opening. Follow the manufacturer's instructions for determining the proper rough opening size for your new skylight.

With standard rafter-frame roof construction, you can safely cut into one or two rafters as long as you permanently support the cut rafters. If your house has a truss roof, the skylight needs to fit between two trusses. Never alter your roof trusses to accommodate a wider skylight by cutting or removing parts of their framework. If your house has a heavy slate or clay tile roof, talk with an architect or building engineer regarding how to reinforce the new framing.

If you install your skylight facing west or south it will receive the greatest amount of direct sunlight, but the flip side is that the intensity of the light could overheat your space. For that reason, you may want to position it facing east or north for cooler room lighting. Since installing a skylight requires working on the roof, carefully set up ladders and wear fall-arresting gear. The job will go more smoothly and safely with a helper.

How to Install a Skylight

Frame the rough opening for the skylight according to the size specifications provided with the unit. Skylights are sized so they fit between 24 or 16" on-center roof members, so if you have chosen a model wisely, you only need to install a header and a sill to complete the rough framing. In uninsulated garages, single 2 × 4s may be used for the rough frame. In a cathedral ceiling, or a skylight shaft, use the same width dimensional lumber as the rafters.

Option: If your skylight unit is narrower than the opening between the king studs, measure and make marks for the trimmers: They should be centered in the opening and spaced according to the manufacturer's specifications. Cut the trimmers from the same 2× lumber used for the rest of the frame, and nail them in place with 10d common nails. Remove the 2 × 4 braces.

Mark the cutout area for the roof sheathing by driving a long deck screw or a casing nail at each corner of the framed opening on the interior side.

Outline the roof cutout by snapping chalk lines between the points of the deck screws driven at the corners of the opening. Be sure to follow good safety practices for working on roofs: wear shoes with nonskid soles, such as tennis shoes, and use roof jacks and fall-arresting gear on roofs with a pitch greater than 4-in-12. Also be aware of weather conditions.

Cut out the roof opening. Mount an old blade in a circular saw or cordless trim saw and plunge cut along the top and bottom cutting lines. Stop short of the corners so you don't overcut. Before making the side cuts, tack a long 1 × 4 across the opening, perpendicular to the top and bottom cuts, driving a couple of screws through the 1 × 4 and into the cutout area. The 1 × 4 will keep the waste from falling into the house through the hole. Make the side cuts and then finish the cuts at the corners with a jigsaw or reciprocating saw.

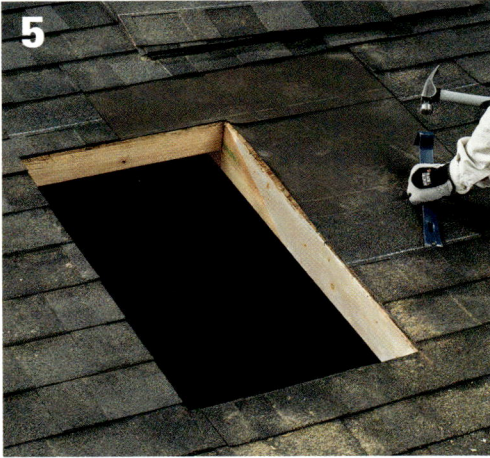

5

Remove the shingles surrounding the opening, but try not to rip the building paper beneath. Salvage the shingles if you can so they can be reinstalled (they'll match better than new shingles). Start with the row of shingles above the opening. Once these are removed you'll have access to the roofing nails on lower courses.

6

Seal the bottom of the rough frame opening. Apply a strip of self-adhesive flashing at the bottom of the roof opening to create a seal on the curb and to cover the seam between the underlayment and the roof deck. This is for extra protection.

7

Position the skylight in the opening. Different models use different fastening and centering devices. The one seen here is installed using pairs of adjustable brackets that are fastened to the roof deck and to the sides of the skylight frame.

8

Fasten the skylight unit. Many models employ adjustable brackets like the ones seen here so the skylight can be raised or lowered and centered in the opening. The brackets seen here have a slot and several nail holes in the horizontal flange. Drive a roofing nail in all four slots and then shift the unit side to side as necessary until it is centered in the opening. The brackets also allow the unit to be raised or lowered so the bottom edges of the cladding are the recommended distance above the finished roof surface (see manufacturer's recommendations).

Install self-adhesive flashing strips around the skylight curb. Start with the base strip, cutting slits in the corners so the flashing extends all the way up the curb (you'll need to remove metal cladding strips first). Install the head flashing last so all strips overlap from above.

Install the metal flashing beginning with the sill. Some skylights have a 4-piece flashing kit where the side flashing is simply shingled over. Others, like the one seen here, include solid base and head flashing components and step flashing that is woven in with the shingles as the roof coverings are installed.

Replace shingles up to the skylight curb. Install shingles in complete rows, notching them to fit around the curb. Stop once the granular surfaces of the top row of shingles meet the curb.

Install side flashing. Here, metal step flashing is interwoven with the shingles. Make sure that the horizontal tabs on the step flashing are all covered with shingles. Attach step flashing to skylight with one nail per piece, but don't nail flashing to the roof.

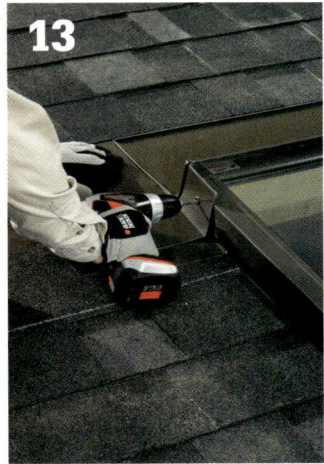

Install the head flashing piece so it overlaps the last course of shingle and step flashing. Finish shingling in the installation area, again taking care not to nail through any metal flashing. Replace the metal cladding and caulk if recommended by the manufacturer.

Entry Doors

Entry doors also qualify for the tax credit of 30% of the product cost. Like windows, doors must have an SHGC and U value of 0.30 (or other criteria listed at energystar.gov) and you'll need to replace the entire door, including the door frame. Most types of doors can qualify – glass, metal, wood or fiberglass doors can qualify whether they're front doors, back doors or garage service doors (as long as the garage is insulated). Doors with sidelights or fixed panels can qualify, as can sliding doors, French doors or full glass entry doors. However, entry handles and locks are not included in the tax credit.

If you are replacing a single entry door with a double door or a door with a sidelight or sidelights, you will need to enlarge the door opening. Be sure to file your plans with your local building department and obtain a permit. You'll need to provide temporary support from the time you remove the wall studs in the new opening until you've installed and secured a new door header that's approved for the new span distance.

The American Craftsman style door with sidelights installed in this project has the look and texture of a classic wood door, but it is actually created from fiberglass. Properly finished fiberglass doors are quite convincing in their ability to replicate wood grain, while still offering the durability and low maintenance of fiberglass.

After

Before

Replacing an old, leaky entry door with a beautiful new upgrade has a high payback in increased curb appeal and energy savings, and it qualifies for a tax credit.

How to Replace an Entry Door

1

If the new door or system is wider than the old entry door, mark the edges of the larger rough opening onto the wall surface. If possible, try to locate the new opening so one edge will be against an existing wall stud. Be sure to include the thickness of the new framing you'll need to add when removing the wall coverings. Remove the old entry door by cutting through the fasteners driven into the jamb with a reciprocating saw.

2

Frame in the new rough opening for the replacement door (see pages 28 to 29). The instructions that come with the door will recommend a rough opening size, which is usually sized to create a ½" gap between the door and the studs and header. Remove siding as needed (see page 37).

3

Cut door drip cap to fit the width of the opening and tuck the back edge up behind the wallcovering at the top of the door opening. Attach the drip cap with caulk only.

4

Apply heavy beads of caulk to the underside of the door sill and to the subfloor in the sill installation area. Use plenty of caulk. Unpack the door unit and set it in the rough opening to make sure it fits correctly. Remove it. Add flashing tape at the base and sides.

5

Set the door sill in the threshold and raise the unit up so it fits cleanly in the opening, with the exterior trim flush against the wall sheathing. Press down on the sill to seat it in the caulk and wipe up any squeeze-out with a damp rag.

6

Use a level to make sure the unit is plumb and then tack it to the rough opening studs using nails driven through the brickmold. On single, hinged doors, drive the nails just above the hinge locations. *Note: Many door installers prefer deck screws over nails when attaching the jambs. Screws offer more gripping strength and are easier to adjust, but covering the screw heads is more difficult than filling nail holes.*

7

Drive wood shims between the jamb and the wall studs near the top and bottom and at hinge locations. Locate the shims directly above the pairs of nails you drove. Doublecheck the door with the level to make sure it is still plumb.

8

Drive shims at the top and bottom and near the top. Only drive the nails part way. Test for plumb again. Check to make sure the door opens and closes evenly, without binding. Fill the gap around the door with minimal expanding foam, then add casings.

To remove a piece of wood siding, start by prying up the piece above using a flat pry bar near the nail locations. Knock the top piece back down with a hammer to expose the raised nails, then pull the nails. Insert spacers between the siding and sheathing to make it easier to access the work areas. Use a hacksaw or reciprocating saw to shear any difficult nails.

Siding shown cut away for clarity

Vinyl and metal siding pieces have a locking J-channel that fits over the bottom of the nailing strip on the piece below. Use a zip tool (inset) to separate siding panels. Insert the zip tool at the overlapping seam nearest the removal area. Slide the zip tool over the J-channel, pulling outward slightly to unlock the joint from the siding below. Remove nails from the panel, then push the panel down to unlock it.

Measure, cut, and install undersill beneath each window on vinyl-sided houses. The undersill should be flush with the outside lip of the J-channel on the sides.

For wood or cement board siding, slide the siding panel against the bottom window trim. Mark the panel ⅛" from the outside edges of the side trim. Place a scrap piece of siding next to the window trim at the proper overlap. Mark the depth of the cut ⅛" below the bottom trim. Transfer the measurement to the siding panel and cut it to fit. Install the cutout panel around the window.

Patio Doors

A sliding or swingout patio door allows several times the amount of natural light into a room that a single door lets in, and either type can qualify for a tax credit.

When choosing a new patio door you'll need to decide between a model with a hinged door or one with a sliding door panel. Both types use the same installation techniques. Swinging doors tend to require less maintenance than sliding doors, and they offer better security. Sliding doors are a good choice if ventilation is one of your requirements because the amount of air they let in is easy to regulate. You can also leave a sliding door open without the wind catching it and causing it to slam or break.

Enlarging a door opening requires that you make structural changes to your house, so it almost always requires a building permit. During construction you will need to provide temporary support to replace the bearing being done by the wall studs you'll need to cut. And when you install the new door the framed opening must have a substantial header. Check with your local building department for the header requirements. In ceilings that are shorter than eight feet, such as basements, you may need to use a header that's fabricated from engineered beams to meet the load-bearing requirements within the available space.

Before

After

Replacing a single door with a sliding patio door is a great way to add light to a walkout basement and create an inviting entryway into your home.

How to Install a Patio Door

Build a temporary support wall. Use doubled 2 x 4s (or 4 x 4s) for the top plate and support posts. The wall should extend at least 2 ft. past the planned door opening in each direction and cannot be more than 24" away from the bearing wall. Make sure it's plumb, and shim it tightly to the joist in the ceiling.

Remove the old door and the wallcoverings in the project area. If there are light switches or receptacles in the demolition area, shut off their power supply at the main service panel and then remove cover plates. To remove the old door, take off the case molding and then cut through the nails by sawing between the jambs and the frame with a reciprocating saw and nail-cutting blades (inset).

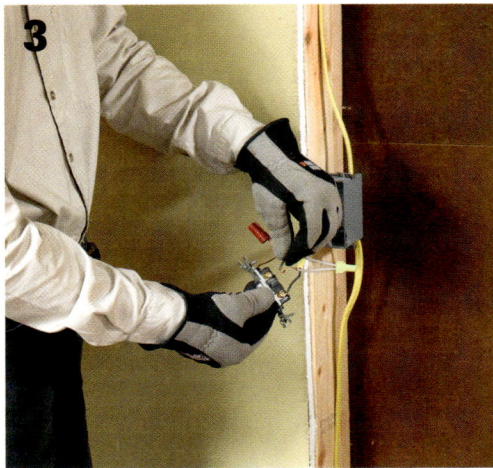

Relocate wiring elements such as switches and receptacles so they are safely outside the new door area. You will need an electrical permit for this and an on-site inspection. If you are not experienced with home wiring, hire an electrician for this part of the job.

Remove wall studs in the project area. If they are difficult to remove, cut them through the center with a reciprocating saw first. Watch out for nails driven in through the exterior side.

Frame the rough opening so it is sized according to the door manufacturer's recommendation. Install the new king studs if needed and then install the jack studs.

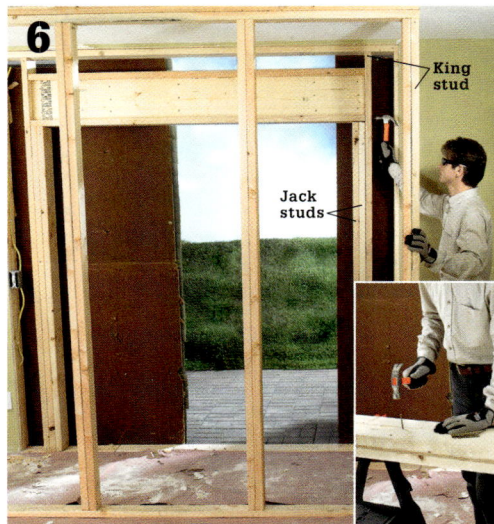

King stud

Jack studs

Install the new header by driving 16d nails through the king stud and into the ends of the header. You can make your own structural header by sandwiching a strip of ½" plywood between two pieces of dimensional lumber (inset). Assemble the header with construction adhesive and 10d nails or 2½" deck screws. You can also purchase an engineered header.

Cut through the exterior wall materials. You can either mark the corners of the framed opening by driving a nail out from the side, or simply use the framed opening as guidance for your reciprocating saw. Also cut through the sole plate at the edges of the opening so the cut end is flush with the jack stud face.

Lift the door unit or frame into the opening with a helper. Test the fit. Trace the edges of the preattached brickmold onto the outside wall, or place a piece of brickmold next to the door and trace around the perimeter to establish cutting lines (inset). Remove the door.

9

Cut along the brickmold cutting lines with a saw set to a cutting depth equal to the thickness of the siding on siding sides. Finish the cuts at the corners with a handsaw. Thoroughly vacuum the floor in the door opening.

10

Seal the framed opening by installing strips of building paper or self-adhesive rubber flashing product. Make sure that the top strip overlaps any seams you create. If the patio door is exposed, insert drip edge molding under the siding at the top.

11

Apply a bead of exterior-rated caulk to the door threshold. Also apply caulk to the back surface of the preattached brickmold or the nailing flange (whichever your door has).

12

Position the door so the brickmold or nailing flange is tight against the siding on both sides. Tack the door near the top of each side and then check with a level. Install shims where necessary so the door is plumb. Re-hang the door in the frame, if it has been removed.

13

Fill the gaps around the door with minimal expanding foam or with loosely backed fiberglass insulation (foam makes a better seal). Patch the wall and attach case molding (see page 25). If your door does not have preattached brickmold, cut and attach molding on the outside.

Garage Doors

Garage doors bear the brunt of everything Mother Nature and an active household throw at them—seasonal temperature swings, moisture, buffeting winds, blistering sunlight, or a badly misfired half-court jump shot. If the time has come to replace yours, you can qualify for the 30 percent tax credit if you purchase an insulated door with a U value and SHGC of 0.30 or less and your garage is insulated. Even if your garage is detached, you can still qualify as long as the garage is fully insulated.

Door manufacturers provide many options for cladding colors, panel layout and texture, exterior hardware, and window styles. New garage doors, such as the fiberglass and steel model shown here, also benefit from improved material construction, more sophisticated safety features, and enhanced energy efficiency. To find a door that qualifies for the credit, look for labels or contact the manufacturer.

Replacing a garage door is surprisingly straightforward and safe. If you have moderate tool skills and a helper or two, you should have little difficulty removing an old door and replacing it with a new one in a single day. Garage door kits come with all the necessary hardware and detailed instructions. Generally, you won't have to modify the door opening once the old door is removed in order to install a new one. And, most garage door openers can be retrofitted to a new door with a few minor adjustments.

Tough Tax Credit Questions ▸

Wondering if a garage door for your insulated barn qualifies? For answers to these and other questions, go to energystar.gov, to the Tax Credits for Energy Efficiency page. Open the Frequently Asked Questions feature and look for the "Ask a Question" button in the menu bar.

After

Before

A failing garage door not only detracts from the appearance of your home, it can be a real headache. Install an energy efficient door and you can save 30% of the materials cost through a tax credit.

How to Remove a Garage Door

With the garage door lowered, remove the clevis pin or bolt and nut that connects the garage door opener trolley arm to the garage door. Then activate the garage door opener to move the trolley to the rear of the track.

With the door fully raised, attach locking pliers or a clamp on the door track underneath the door's bottom rollers. Do this on both door tracks. The pliers or clamp will prevent the door from falling when you remove the extension springs.

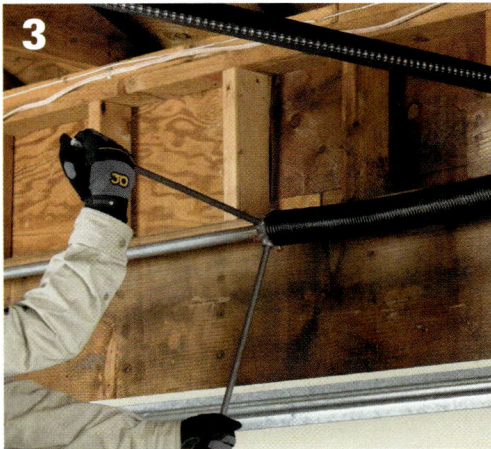

Release the tension in the door spring or springs. If your opener has an extension spring in each channel, you simply need to unhook and remove them with the door open. If your opener operates with torsion springs, like the one shown here, you'll need a special tool called a winding bar to unwind the spring. But be aware that this is a very dangerous job (see warning box, right) and it is recommended that you hire a professional garage door installer to do it.

Warning: Beware of Torsion Springs ▶

Winding and unwinding torsion springs is a very risky task for do-it-yourselfers and it is recommended that you hire a garage door installer for this part of the job. These heavy coils are installed parallel to the door header instead of in the track channels, like lighter-weight extension springs. Torsion springs hold massive amounts of energy and can easily throw a tool if they slip during the winding or unwinding process. When installed, the spring is wound with a winding bar that fits into lugs that are attached to the loose ends of the springs. The installer counts a prescribed number of turns to get the correct spring tension and then affixes the plug to the cylinder with a set screw or bolt. The manual for your door will contain the requirements for your torsion spring. If you choose to proceed with the project yourself, you can rent a winding bar at a garage door installation company. Never substitute a metal dowel, screwdriver, or any other tool for a genuine winding bar that's shaped to fit the lugs on your door.

With the help of another person, remove both locking pliers from the door tracks and carefully lower the old door to the floor. Be aware that, without springs installed, you'll bear the entire weight of the door as you lower it. Garage doors can weigh 200 to 400 lbs., so use extreme caution.

Starting at the top panel, unbolt the top hinges and door roller hardware and lift the top door section out of the tracks. Repeat for the other sections, removing only one section's hardware at a time. After you have removed all door sections, unbolt both track assemblies from the door jambs and dismantle the tracks. These can be discarded. Do not remove the perforated hanger brackets that hold the rear end of the tracks to the ceiling framing or roof trusses. Unless these are damaged, they can usually be reused for the new door tracks.

How to Install a Garage Door

Measure the inside opening of the doorway, the headroom clearance to the ceiling, and the width of the existing top header. Check these measurements against the minimum requirements outlined in the instruction manual that comes with your new door. Depending on the design of the new door and spring system, you may need to first install a wider header or make other modifications to your framing or garage door opener height to accommodate the new door.

Working on the floor, assemble the vertical tracks, jamb brackets, and flag angle hardware. Install the roller and hinge hardware on the bottom door section.

3

Check the top of the door section for level. After you have set the bottom door section into position against the side jambs, adjust it left or right until the side jambs overlap it evenly. Place shims beneath the door, if necessary, to level it. Have a helper hold the door section in place against the jambs until it is secured in the tracks.

4

Slip the left vertical track over the door section rollers and against the side jamb. Adjust it for plumb, then fasten the jamb brackets to the side jamb with lag screws. Carefully measure, mark, and install the right vertical track now as well.

5

Depending on your door design, you may need to attach lift cables to the bottom door section at this time. Follow the instructions that come with your door to connect these cables correctly

6

Fasten the end and intermediate hinges to the bottom door section, and then install roller brackets and hinges to the other door sections. Attach hinges to the top edges of each door section only. This way, you'll be able to stack one section on top of the next during assembly.

Connect the bottom hinges to the second door section after you have slipped the second door section into place in the door tracks and on top of the first section. Repeat the process until you have installed all but the top door section.

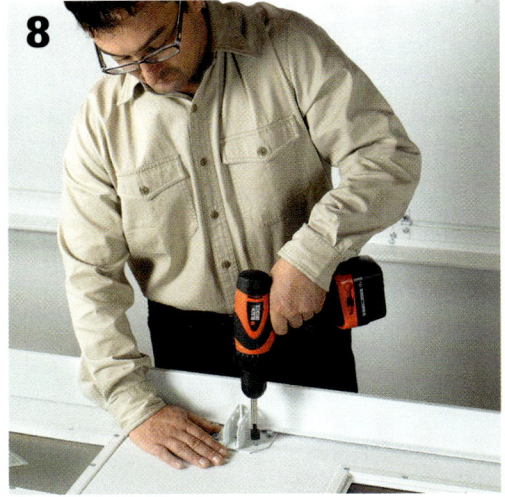

The top door section may require special top roller brackets, additional bracing, and a bracket for securing a garage door opener. Install these parts now, following the door manufacturer's instructions.

Set the top door section in place and fasten it to the hinges below it. Hold it in place temporarily with a few nails driven at an angle up into the top door header.

Fasten horizonal door tracks to the flag angle brackets on top of the vertical tracks. Check the horizontal tracks for level, and inspect their rear connection points to the hanger brackets you left from the previous door. *Note: If you need to modify or replace the old hanger brackets, do this now and connect the horizontal tracks to the brackets to complete the track installation. Do not attempt to open the new door.*

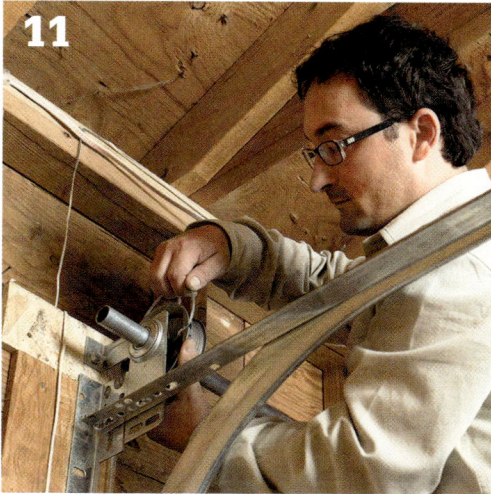

11

Assemble the torsion spring components and mount any required support brackets to the top door jamb. Set the torsion spring into place on its jamb brackets and fasten it. Secure the winding cables to the spring winding drums (see Warning, page 43).

12

Attach a locking pliers or clamp to each door track to prevent the door from raising when you wind the counterbalance springs. Follow the instructions that come with your door kit to wind each torsion spring correctly. You need winding bars to do this. You can rent or borrow these bars from a garage door dealer or installer.

13

Attach the door's emergency disconnect handle, door lock, lift handles, and other hardware, depending on your door kit. Before fully raising the door, carefully check the alignment of the door tracks to one another and the spacing between the door and tracks. Adjust the roller brackets, if needed.

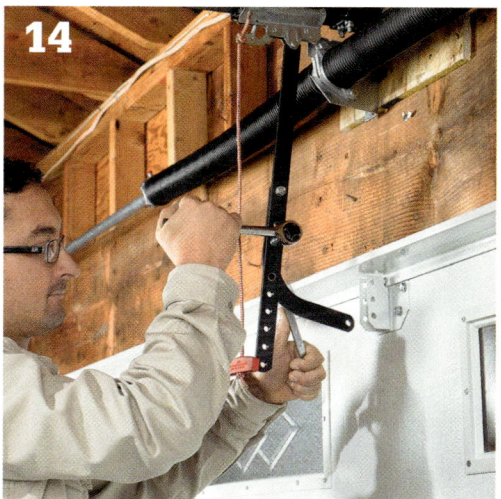

14

Attach the garage door opener trolley arm to the door's operator bracket. You may need to adjust the length of the arm by changing the arrangement of the parts to retrofit it to the new door. Test the action and travel of the new door and then install an electric garage door opener (optional). Finally, measure, cut, and nail stop moldings in place and add a garage door sweep.

Some roof coverings are eligible for the federal tax credit program. Asphalt shingles need to be in the mid-tone to light color range to qualify.

ROOFING

A new roof is a major, long-term investment, with materials alone starting at several thousand dollars in cost, even for a small roof. By choosing a roofing material that qualifies for the energy-efficiency tax credits, you can earn a tax credit of up to $1,500 and substantially reduce that cost. Unlike windows or water heaters, the roofing material you choose doesn't necessarily have to be a more expensive type. It just has to be more reflective, which often just means lighter-colored.

Roofing materials that are more reflective save energy by lowering roof temperatures, reducing the amount of heat transmitted into the house and thus reducing cooling costs. This is especially significant in the warmer parts of the country where attics are often not as heavily insulated and air conditioning is a major part of energy use. Reflective roofing materials also help lower overall temperatures in densely populated areas where thousands of dark roofs can actually add several degrees to the local climate—a big part of the reason cities feel hotter than the surrounding countryside.

Energy Star-qualified roofs must meet basic standards for reflectivity, and any metal or asphalt roofing product with the Energy Star designation automatically qualifies for the energy tax credit. You can find links to approved products at energystar.gov, or just ask at your local supplier. Most manufacturers have at least a few products that qualify, so finding one that you like for your roof shouldn't be a problem. It's probably not worth tearing off a good roof to put a lighter roof on, but if you're planning on re-roofing in the next few years—the tax credits are available in 2009 and 2010—there's little reason not to reduce your costs by finding a color that qualifies for the credit.

Qualification

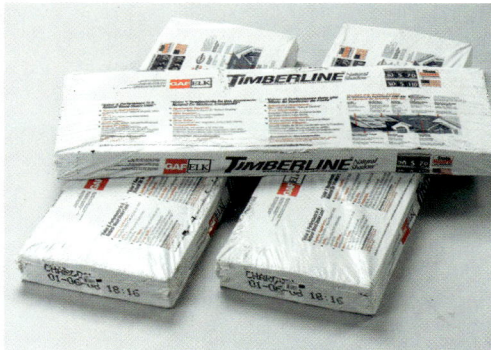

Any metal or asphalt roof with an Energy Star designation and a Manufacturer Certification Statement qualifies for the tax credit. The credit is for 30 percent of the material cost only, not including labor, from 2009 to 2010. At this point only metal or asphalt shingles are covered, but other materials may qualify in the future, so check with the manufacturer or energystar.gov before buying.

Energy savings from installing an Energy Star roof can be estimated with an online calculator (available at roofcalc.com). However, these savings will not be significant if you have a well-insulated roof or use minimal air conditioning.

Some concrete, clay, rubber, and coated roofs have also received Energy Star designations, but are not yet included in the tax credit program. Check with the manufacturer or energystar.gov for information on these types. Wood and slate shingles and translucent panels do not qualify.

Asphalt roofing shingles qualify if they have an Energy Star designation. Generally these are light- to medium-colored shingles in a variety of styles.

Roofing Product Criteria ▶

Low slope roofs (2/12 slope or less):	Initial solar reflectance >= 0.65 Reflectance after 3 years >= 0.50
Steep slope roofs (over 2/12 slope):	Initial solar reflectance >= 0.25 Reflectance after 3 years >= 0.15

Roll roofing, which is used on low slope roofs, will qualify if it has an Energy Star designation.

Metal roofs also qualify, and hundreds of different colors and styles are available that have earned Energy Star designations.

Materials & Tools

Roofing materials are ordered in squares, with one square equaling 100 square feet. To determine how many squares are needed, first figure out the square footage of your roof. The easiest way to make this calculation is to multiply the length by the width of each section of roof, and then add the numbers together.

For steep roofs and those with complex designs, do your measuring from the ground and multiply by a number based on the slope of your roof. Measure the length and width of your house, include the overhangs, then multiply the numbers together to determine the overall square footage. Using the chart at the lower right, multiply the square footage by a number based on the roof's slope. Add 10 percent for waste, then divide the total square footage by 100 to determine the number of squares you need. Don't spend time calculating and subtracting the areas that won't be covered, such as skylights and chimneys. They're usually small enough that they don't impact the number of squares you need. Besides, it's good to have extra materials for waste, mistakes, and later repairs.

To determine how much flashing you'll need, measure the length of the valley to figure valley flashing, the lengths of the eaves and rakes to figure drip edge, and the number and size of vent pipes to figure vent flashing.

Specialty roofing tools include roof jacks (A) for use on steep roofs, a roofing shovel (B) for tearoff work, a pneumatic nailer (C), a utility knife with hooked blade (D) for trimming shingles, a roofing hammer with alignment guides and hatchet blade (E) for shingle installation, and a magnet for site cleanup (F).

Calculate the roof's surface by multiplying the height of the roof by the width. Do this for each section, then add the totals together. Divide that number by 100, add 10 percent for waste, and that's the number of squares of roofing materials you need.

Conversion Chart			
Slope	Multiply by	Slope	Multiply by
2 in 12	1.02	8 in 12	1.20
3 in 12	1.03	9 in 12	1.25
4 in 12	1.06	10 in 12	1.30
5 in 12	1.08	11 in 12	1.36
6 in 12	1.12	12 in 12	1.41
7 in 12	1.16		

Rolled flashing material

Drip edge

Preformed valley flashing

Aviation snips

Vent pipe flashing

Step flashing blanks

Skylight flashing kit (partial)

Roof flashing can be hand cut or purchased in preformed shapes and sizes. Long pieces of valley flashing, base flashing, top saddles, and other nonstandard pieces can be cut from rolled flashing material using aviation snips. Step flashing blanks can be bought in standard sizes and bent to fit. Drip edge and vent pipe flashing are available preformed. Skylight flashing usually comes as a kit with the window. Complicated flashings, such as chimney crickets, can be custom-fabricated by a metalworker.

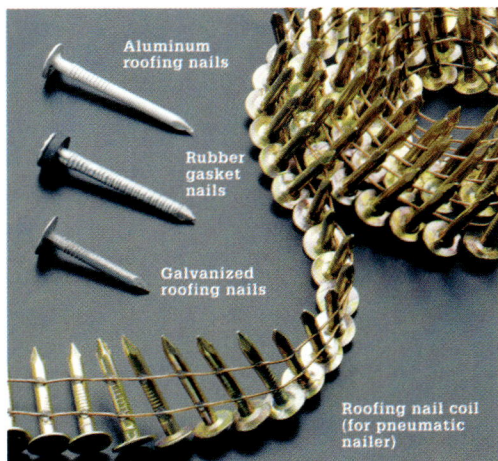

Aluminum roofing nails

Rubber gasket nails

Galvanized roofing nails

Roofing nail coil (for pneumatic nailer)

Different fasteners are specially developed for different jobs. Use galvanized roofing nails to hand nail shingles; use aluminum nails for aluminum flashing; use rubber gasket nails for galvanized metal flashing; and use nail coils for pneumatic nailers.

Felt paper (30#)

Roofing cement

Ice-guard membrane

Common roofing materials include 30# felt paper for use as underlayment; ice-guard membrane for use as underlayment in cold climates; and tubes of roofing cement for sealing small holes, cracks, and joints.

For more secure footing, fashion a roofing ladder by nailing wood strips across a pair of 2 × 4s. Secure the ladder to the roof jacks, and use it to maintain your footing.

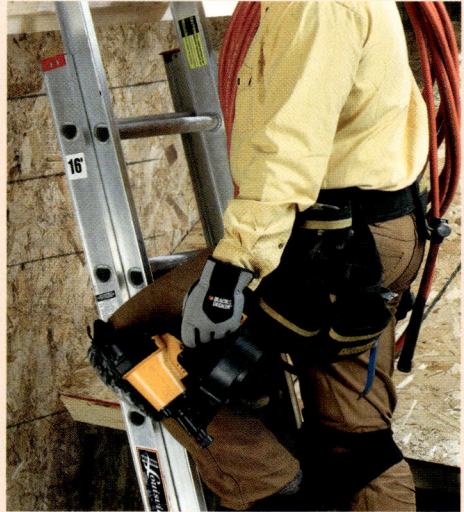

Never climb a ladder with a loaded air nailer attached to a pressurized air hose. Even with trigger safeties, air guns pose a serious danger to the operator as well as anyone who may be standing near the ladder.

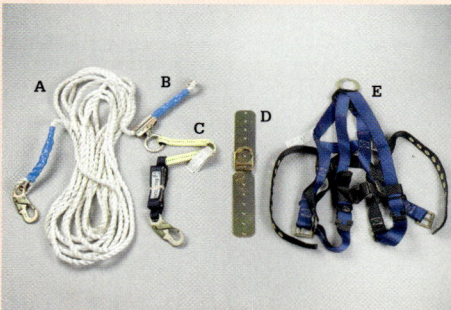

On step roofs, use personal fall-arresting gear: a lifeline (A) with mechanical rope grab (B) and lanyard (C); a metal ridge anchor (D); and a body harness (E).

For 4-in-12 or steeper roofs, set up roof jacks with a 2 × 8 to create a sturdy work platform on a sloped roof.

Tear-off

Remove the ridge cap using a flat pry bar. Pry up the cap shingles at the nail locations.

Working downward from the peak, tear off the felt paper and old shingles with a roofing shovel or pitchfork.

Unless flashing is in exceptional condition, remove it by slicing through the roofing cement that attaches it to the shingles. You may be able to salvage flashing pieces, such as chimney saddles and crickets, and reuse them.

Pry out any remaining nails, felt paper, and flashing after removing the shingles from the entire tear-off section, and sweep the roof with a broom.

Cover any unshingled sections using tarps weighted down with shingle bundles, if an unexpected delay keeps you from finishing a section before nightfall.

Underlayment & Drip Edge

Place the drip edge with a 45° miter cut at one end of the drip edge using aviation snips along the eaves end of the roof, aligning the mitered end with the rake edge. Nail the drip edge in place every 12".

Overlap pieces of drip edge by 2". Install drip edge across the entire eaves, ending with a mitered cut on the opposite corner.

Install a course of ice and water shield, using the chalk line as a reference and peeling back the protective backing as you unroll it. Snap a chalk line 35⅝" up from the eaves, so the first course of the 36"-wide membrane will overhang the eaves by ⅜". Measuring up from the eaves, make a mark 32" above the top of the last row of underlayment, and snap another chalk line.

Roll out the next course of felt paper (or ice guard, if required) along the chalk line, overlapping the first course by 4". *Tip: Drive staples every 6 to 12" along the edges of felt paper, and one staple per sq. ft. in the field area.*

At valleys, roll felt paper across from both sides, overlapping the ends by 36". Install felt paper up to the ridge—ruled side up—snapping horizontal lines every two or three rows to check alignment. Overlap horizontal seams by 4", vertical seams by 12", and hips and ridges by 6". Trim the courses flush with the rake edges.

Install a piece of drip edge with a 45° miter cut in along the rake edge, forming a miter joint with the drip edge along the eaves. Overlap pieces by 2", making sure the higher piece is on top at the overlap. Apply drip edge all the way to the peak. Install drip edge along the other rake edges the same way.

Preparation Tips

Starting at the eaves, set a piece of valley flashing into the valley so the bottom of the V rests in the crease of the valley. Nail the flashing at 12" intervals along each side. Trim the end of the flashing at the eaves so it's flush with the drip edge at each side. Working toward the top of the valley, add flashing pieces so they overlap by at least 8" until you reach the ridge.

Let the top edge of the flashing extend a few inches beyond the ridge. Bend the flashing over the ridge so it lies flat on the opposite side of the roof. If you're installing preformed flashing, make a small cut in the spine for easier bending. Cover nail heads with roofing cement (unless you're using rubber gasket nails). Apply roofing cement along the side edges of the flashing.

Layout Planning

Stagger shingles for effective protection against leaks. If the tab slots are aligned in successive rows, water forms channels, increasing erosion of the mineral surface of the shingles. Creating a 6" offset between rows of shingles—with the three-tab shingles shown above—ensures that the tab slots do not align.

Shingling

Snap a chalk line onto the ice guard 11½" up from the eaves edge to mark the alignment of the starter course. This will result in a ½" shingle overhang for standard 12" shingles. Trim off one-half (6") of an end tab on a shingle. *Tip: Use blue chalk rather than red. Red chalk will stain roofing materials.*

Position the trimmed shingle upside down, so the tabs are aligned with the chalk line and the half-tab is flush against the rake edge. Drive ⅞" roofing nails near each end, 1" down from each slot between tabs. Butt a full upside-down shingle next to the trimmed shingle, and nail it. Fill out the row, trimming the last shingle flush with the opposite rake edge.

Apply the first full course of shingles over the starter course with the tabs pointing down. Begin at the rake edge where you began the starter row. Place the first shingle so it overhangs the rake edge by ⅜" and the eaves edge by ½". Make sure the top of each shingle is flush with the top of the starter course, following the chalk line.

Snap a chalk line from the eaves edge to the ridge to create a vertical line to align the shingles. Choose an area with no obstructions, as close as possible to the center of the roof. The chalk line should pass through a slot or a shingle edge on the first full shingle course. Use a carpenter's square to establish a line perpendicular to the eaves edge.

Use the vertical reference line to establish a shingle pattern with slots that are offset by 6" in succeeding courses. Tack down a shingle 6" to one side of the vertical line and 5" above the bottom edge of the first-course shingles to start the second row. Tack down shingles for the third and fourth courses, 12" and 18" from the vertical line. Butt the fifth course against the line

Check the alignment of the shingles after each four-course cycle. In several spots on the last installed course, measure from the bottom edge of a shingle to the nearest felt paper line. If you discover any misalignment, make minor adjustments over the next few rows until it's corrected.

When you reach obstructions, such as dormers, install a full course of shingles above them so you can retain your shingle offset pattern. On the unshingled side of the obstruction, snap another vertical reference line using the shingles above the obstruction as a guide.

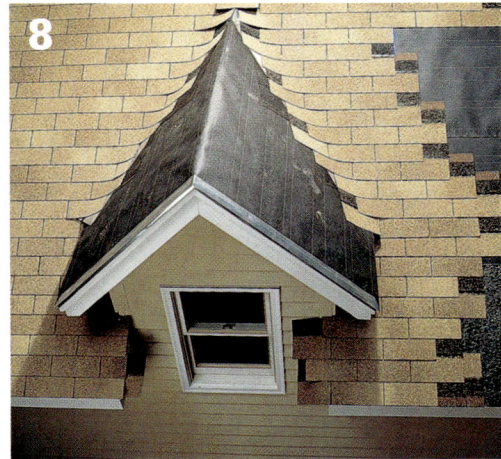

Shingle upward from the eaves on the unshingled side of the obstruction using the vertical line as a reference for re-establishing your shingle slot offset pattern. Fill out the shingle courses past the rake edges of the roof, then trim off the excess.

Trim off excess shingle material at the V in the valley flashing using a utility knife and straightedge. Do not cut into the flashing. The edges will be trimmed back farther at a slight taper after both roof decks are completely shingled.

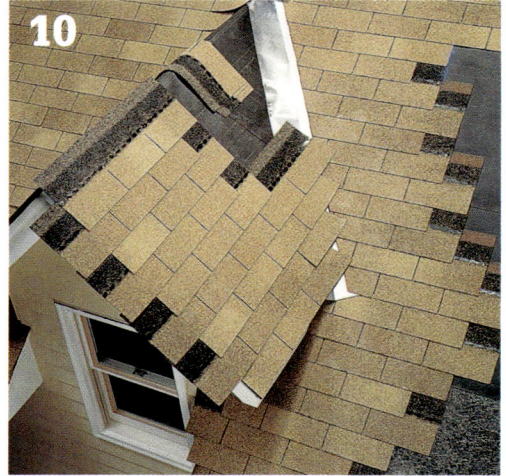

Install shingles on adjoining roof decks, starting at the bottom edge using the same offset alignment pattern shown in steps 1 to 6. Install shingles until courses overlap the center of the valley flashing. Trim shingles at both sides of the valley when finished.

To install vent pipe flashing, apply a heavy double bead of roofing cement along the edges of the flange. The flashing rests on at least one row of shingles, installed up to the vent pipe.

Cut shingles to fit around the neck of the flashing so they lie flat against the flange. Do not drive roofing nails through the flashing. Instead, apply roofing cement to the back of shingles where they lie over the flashing.

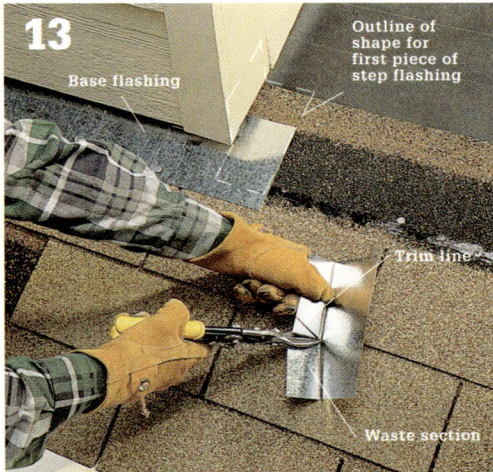

13
Base flashing

Outline of shape for first piece of step flashing

Trim line

Waste section

Cut the step flashing to fit. Mark a trim line on the flashing, following the vertical edge of the element. Shingle up to an element that requires flashing so the top of the reveal areas are within 5" of the element. Install base flashing using the old base flashing as a template. Bend a piece of step flashing in half and set it next to the lowest corner of the element.

14
Spacer

Pry out the lowest courses of siding and any trim at the base of the element. Insert spacers to prop the trim or siding away from the work area. Apply roofing cement to the base flashing in the area where the overlap with the step flashing will be formed. Tuck the trimmed piece of step flashing under the propped area, and secure the flashing. Fasten the flashing with one rubber gasket nail driven near the top and into the roof deck.

15

Apply roofing cement to the top side of the first piece of step flashing where it will be covered by the next shingle course. Install the shingle by pressing it firmly into the roofing cement. Do not nail through the flashing underneath.

16

Tuck another piece of flashing under the trim or siding, overlapping the first piece of flashing at least 2". Set the flashing into roofing cement applied on the top of the shingle. Nail the shingle in place without driving nails through the flashing. Install flashing up to the top of the element the same way. Trim the last piece of flashing to fit the top corner of the element. Reattach the siding and trim.

17

Counterflashing

Base flashing

To install flashing around a chimney, press the base flashing into the roofing cement and bend the flashing around the edges. Drive rubber gasket nails through the flashing flange into the roof deck. Shingle up to the chimney base. Use the old base flashing as a template to cut new flashing. Bend up the counter flashing. Apply roofing cement to the base of the chimney and the shingles just below the base.

18

Step flashing

Install step flashing and shingles, working up to the high side of the chimney. Fasten flashing to the chimney with roofing cement. Fold down the counter flashing as you go.

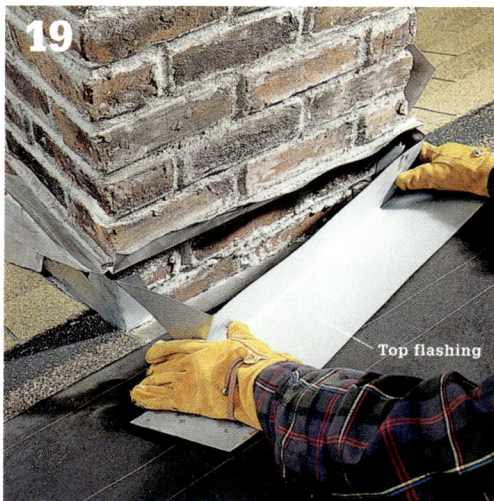

19

Top flashing

Cut and install top flashing (also called a saddle) around the high side of the chimney. Overlap the final piece of flashing along each side. Attach the flashing with roofing cement applied to the deck and chimney and with rubber gasket nails driven through the flashing base into the roof deck. Shingle past the chimney using roofing cement (not nails) to attach shingles over the flashing.

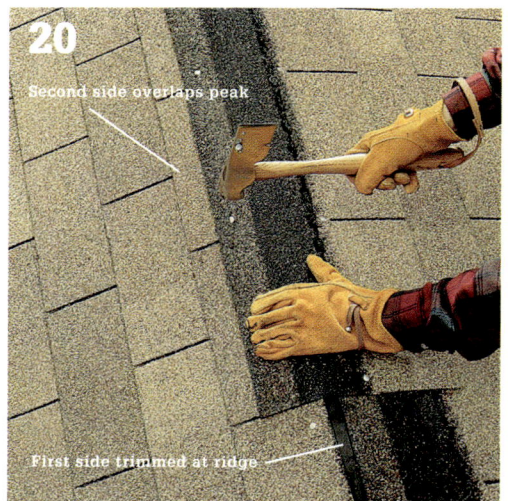

20

Second side overlaps peak

First side trimmed at ridge

When you reach a hip or ridge, shingle up the first side until the top of the uppermost reveal area is within 5" of the hip or ridge. Trim the shingles along the peak. Install shingles on the opposite side of the hip or ridge. Overlap the peak no more than 5".

21

Snap a chalk line 6" down from the ridge, parallel to the peak. Attach cap shingles, starting at one end of the ridge, aligned with the chalk line. Drive two 1¼" roofing nails per cap about 1" from each edge, just below the seal strip.

22

Following the chalk line, install cap shingles halfway along the ridge, creating a 5" reveal for each cap. Then, starting at the opposite end, install caps over the other half of the ridge to meet the first run in the center. Cut a 5"-wide section from the reveal area of a shingle tab, and use it as a "closure cap" to cover the joint where the caps meet.

23

At the valleys, seal the undersides and edges of shingles with roofing cement. Also cover exposed nail heads with roofing cement. After all shingles are installed, trim them at the valleys to create a gap that's 3" wide at the top and widens at a rate of ⅛" per foot as it moves downward. Use a utility knife and straightedge to cut the shingles, making sure not to cut through the valley flashing.

24

Mark and trim the shingles at the rake edges of the roof. Snap a chalk line ⅜" from the edge to make an overhang, then trim the shingles.

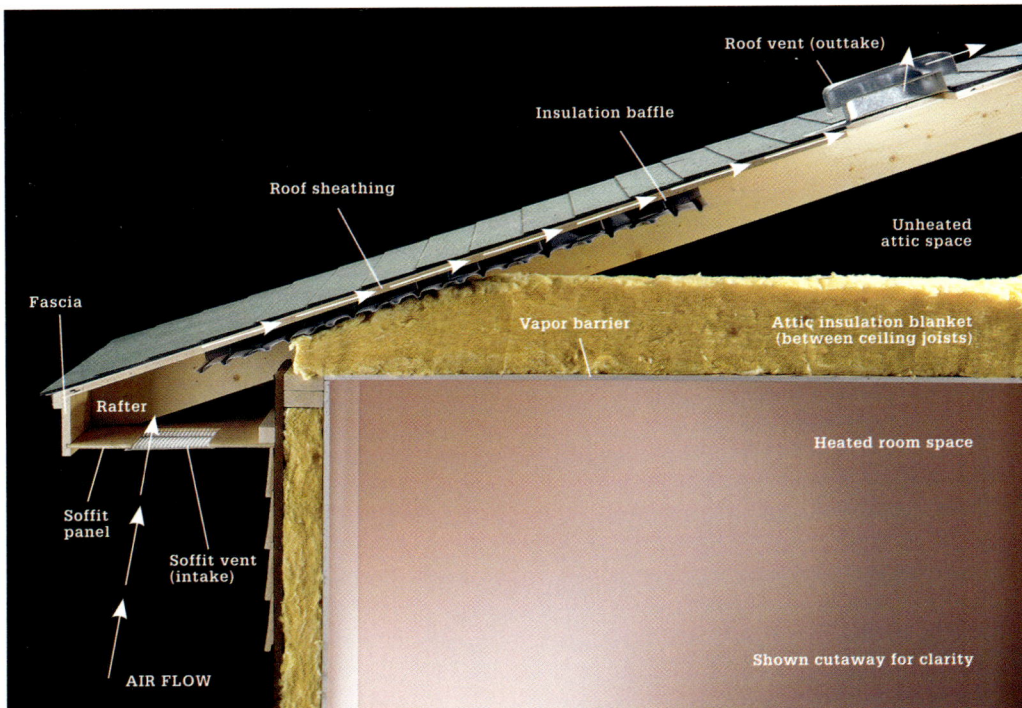

Insulation and weatherizing products of just about every type qualify for the tax credit. When adding insulation, be certain to install vapor barriers or retarders and airflow improvers, including baffles, intake vents, and outtake vents.

INSULATION

Good insulation is the most important component of an energy-efficient home, not to mention the most cost-effective upgrade you can make in your house. Several hundred dollars of insulation in an attic will easily pay for itself in a few years, and it's a simple job that almost anyone can do. Energy-efficiency tax credits will help reduce the price of almost any insulation you buy, making large jobs, like insulating a whole attic or basement or blowing cellulose into the walls, much more affordable.

You can get a credit for 30 percent of the cost of insulation materials, up to $1,500. Labor isn't covered, so if you hire someone to do the work ask them to itemize the material cost. You'll also need the Manufacturer Certification Statement for your tax records. Any type of insulation qualifies, as long as its primary purpose is to insulate, which means

that insulated siding or carpet underlayment would not qualify.

The first step is to evaluate your insulation needs with an energy audit (see page 10). Sealing air leaks with caulk, foam, or weatherstripping is an important part of insulating and should be done as part of an insulation project—unfortunately these materials aren't eligible for the tax credit. If you're installing insulation in an older house, you can usually combine different types. For instance, if you already have loose-fill cellulose insulation between the attic joists, you can roll batts of fiberglass insulation over it, rolling it across the rafters to eliminate any gaps and block heat transfer through the joists. Or, you can blow additional insulation into walls to fill gaps where old insulation has settled, or place rigid insulation over fiberglass in a cathedral ceiling.

The more insulation you have, the better. The chart below shows suggested insulation levels for existing houses, but you don't have to match these levels to qualify for the tax credit. However, if the insulation is going into a new addition or you're converting an unfinished attic or basement to living space, you will need to meet the code requirements for new construction.

Suggested Insulation Levels ▸

Map of DOE's Proposed Climate Zones

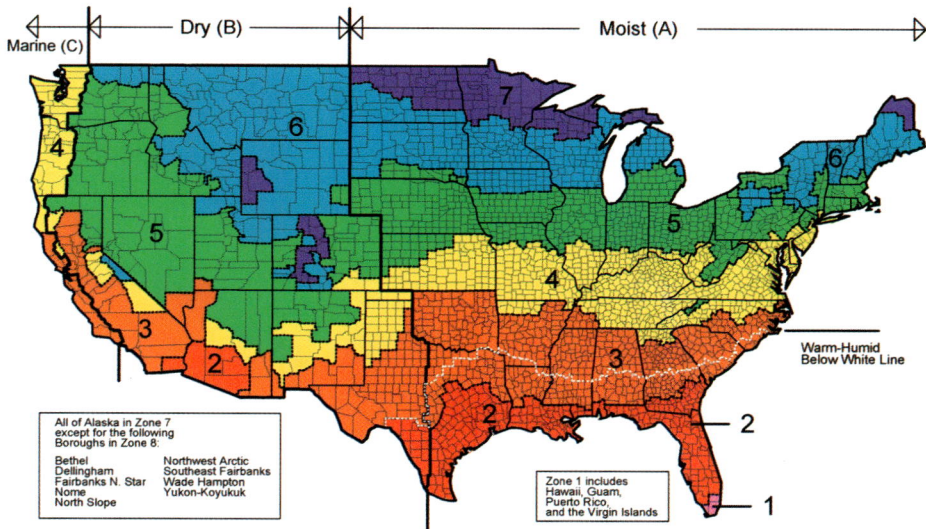

Marine (C) — Dry (B) — Moist (A)

All of Alaska in Zone 7 except for the following Boroughs in Zone 8:

Bethel
Dellingham
Fairbanks N. Star
Nome
North Slope

Northwest Arctic
Southeast Fairbanks
Wade Hampton
Yukon-Koyukuk

Warm-Humid Below White Line

Zone 1 includes Hawaii, Guam, Puerto Rico, and the Virgin Islands

Recommended insulation levels for retrofitting existing wood-framed buildings.

Uninsulated basement or crawl space wall

For Zones 4 to 8: Add R10 (rigid) or R13 (fiberglass).

Insulation for new walls

For Zones 1 to 4: R13

For Zones 5 to 6: R 19

For Zones 7 to 8: R 21

Insulation Types

Insulation improvements in existing homes are typically limited to the attic and the basement or crawlspace. Because the walls in living areas are already covered and finished, adding insulation there requires opening the interior or exterior surfaces. However, if you've determined through an energy audit that your walls are uninsulated or have severely compromised insulation due to settling or other factors, you can have a professional insulator fill the empty wall cavities with blown-in insulation.

Attic insulation is critical to thermal performance for several reasons. Insulation along attic floors (typically in the ceiling framing above the home's top floor) keeps heated air in the living spaces below during the heating season, and it keeps hot attic air from transferring to the living spaces during warmer months. This thermal barrier is especially important in winter, because the chimney effect naturally moves hot air up to upper-floor ceilings where it can easily escape into the attic through conduction or be drawn through air leaks in the ceiling surface. Also, excess heat in an attic space warms up the roof, leading to ice dams in snowy climates.

Most homes, even old ones, have some insulation in their attic. Depending on how much

is there, it might be beneficial to add more insulation, and it's always a good idea to fill in where insulation is insufficient. Adding a blanket of unfaced fiberglass insulation is a common upgrade that homeowners can do themselves. If your attic is vented through soffit vents (under the eaves), make sure the insulation doesn't block airflow underneath the roof deck. If necessary, install insulation baffles to create an air channel above the insulation.

Insulating an unfinished crawlspace or basement is recommended for most homes and climates. If the crawlspace is unheated, it's usually best to insulate between the floor joists to keep heated air inside the first-floor living spaces. In basements, insulate the walls with rigid insulation or a combination of rigid and fiberglass.

Be sure to insulate any water piping that may be susceptible to freezing in cold weather. It's also a good idea to cover bare dirt floors in crawlspaces with a layer of 6-mil polyethylene sheeting to prevent ground moisture from migrating into the space. Check with your local building department for specific insulation and installation recommendations for your area.

Fiberglass batts are affordable and are still the easiest insulation products for DIYers to install. Here, a second layer of fiberglass insulation is being installed perpendicular to the ceiling joists (attic floor joists) to supplement the attic blanket.

Foamed In Place insulation (FIP) is a relatively new product that is normally installed by a crew of professionals. The sticky foam is sprayed into the wall cavity and then trimmed flush with the studs after it expands and dries.

The thermal performance of every type of insulation is shown in its value of resistivity, or R value. The higher the R value, the better the insulation is at slowing heat transfer through conduction. Residential building codes specify recommended R value minimums for all areas of a home's thermal envelope. For help with choosing the right type of insulation for your home, consult with your local building department or a qualified energy auditor or insulation professional. Keep in mind that proper installation is essential for achieving the rated R value of any insulation product.

Here is an overview of the most common types of insulation available:

SPRAYED-FOAM INSULATION

Sprayed-foam, or foamed-in-place, insulation is commonly made with polyurethane foam, though some products are cement-based and some are formulated with soybean oil instead of petroleum products. In existing homes, spray-foam insulation can be used to fill wall cavities through holes in the interior or exterior wall. This must be done by a certified professional installer. It's also used in attics, cathedral ceilings, and throughout the house in new construction.

COTTON

Cotton insulation is often considered a "natural" alternative to traditional fiberglass. It's made primarily from recycled cotton textiles, such as denim, which are treated with borate for insect and moisture resistance and with non-toxic flame retardants. Cotton insulation products include batts, rolls, and loose-fill forms for blow-in applications.

CELLULOSE

Cellulose is a popular green insulation option for several blow-in applications. It's made primarily from recycled newspaper treated with non-toxic borate and/or ammonium sulfate flame retardants. Damp-spray forms (right) are the standard for new construction, while dry, loose-fill versions are used for blow-in applications in attics and for filling wall cavities in existing homes.

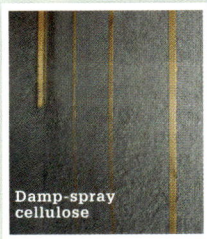

Damp-spray cellulose

FIBERGLASS

By far the most common types of insulation found in American homes are fiberglass batts and rolls. These come in precut strips made to fit between studs, floor joists, rafters, and ceiling joists or truss members. Fiberglass batts are available with or without

Faced fiberglass batts

facings of kraft paper or foil, which serve as a vapor barrier to keep the moisture of hot air out of the framed structure. Vapor barriers are typically installed on the warm-in-winter side of the wall or ceiling. Batts are also available encased in plastic, to contain the glass fibers and eliminate the itchy discomfort of installation. Another form of fiberglass insulation is a loose-fill product used by professionals for blow-in applications in attics.

Conventional forms of fiberglass insulation are made with phenol-formaldehyde binders, but now many manufacturers offer formaldehyde-free products for improved indoor air quality. Look for insulation with Greenguard certification (from the

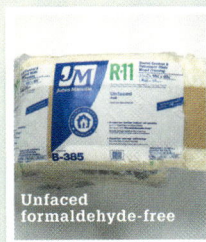

Unfaced formaldehyde-free

Greenguard Environmental Institute) for low emissions.

RIGID FOAM BOARD

Rigid foam panels are widely used to insulate foundation walls and roofs over cathedral ceilings (which often don't have sufficient framing depth for other types of insulation). Three common types are

expanded polystyrene (EPS), polyisocyanurate (ISO, or "polyiso"), and extruded polystyrene (XPS).

Tips for Insulating ▸

Handling fiberglass is a lot more comfortable when you're dressed for it. Wear pants and a long-sleeve shirt, gloves, goggles, and a good-quality dust mask or respirator. Shower as soon as you finish the installation. Never compress insulation to fit into a narrow space.

Use a sharp utility knife to trim the blanket about ¼" wider and longer than the space. To trim, hold the blanket in place and use a wall stud as a straightedge and cutting surface.

Insulate around pipes, wires, and electrical boxes by peeling the blanket in half and sliding the back half behind the obstruction. Then, lay the front half in front of the obstruction. Cut the front half to fit snugly around boxes.

Provide a vapor barrier using faced insulation by tucking along the edges of the insulation until the facing flange is flush with the edge of the framing. Make sure the flanges lie flat, with no wrinkles or gaps, and staple them to the faces of the framing members about every 8". Patch any gaps or facing tears with packing tape or a construction tape supplied by the manufacturer.

Install a polyethylene vapor barrier by draping the sheeting over the entire wall or ceiling, extending it a few inches beyond the perimeter. Staple the sheeting to the framing, and overlap sheets at least 12". Carefully cut around obstructions. Seal around electrical boxes and other penetrations with packing tape. Trim excess sheeting along the ceiling and floor after you install the finish material.

Insulation Comparison ▸

Type	R Value per inch	Relative cost
Fiberglass batts	3.2–3.8	$
Blown-in fiberglass	2.2–2.9	$
Formaldehyde-free batts	3.2	$
Sprayed foam	3.6–7.3	$$–$$$
Cotton	3.2	$$
Cellulose	3.1–3.7	$
Damp-spray cellulose	3.7	$$
Rigid EPS	4.0	$
Rigid ISO	7.0	$$
Rigid XPS	5.0	$$

Insulation Details ▸

Use air-tight electrical boxes for exterior walls and tape them to the vapor barrier to prevent air leaks.

Seal or use special airtight fixtures for exhaust fans and recessed ceiling lights on exterior ceilings—and remember to cover them with insulation.

Seal all wiring or plumbing penetrations between floors and into cold areas with fire-resistant expanding foam.

Seal punctures, tears and seams in the plastic vapor barrier with vapor barrier tape (the type used for housewrap works).

Drafts blowing through gaps in the sheathing can greatly reduce the R value of fiberglass or blown-in insulation. Seal all cracks or consider using sprayed foam insulation, especially if you live in an old house.

Consult local building inspectors about the vapor barrier. Depending on where you live, they may recommend placing it on the inside, the outside, or not using one at all.

FAQ's ▸

Q – Do I have to use a specified R value to qualify for the tax credit?
A – No.

Q – I've had a professional spray the attic rafters with urethane. Can I take 30% of his charges for the tax credit?
A – No, only materials are covered. Ask him to give you a breakdown of his charges.

Q – Do I need a Manufacturer Certification Statement for fiberglass insulation to get the tax credit?
A – Yes. Ask the retailer for one, or download from the manufacturer's web site.

Insulation Tips ▸

- Use rigid polyisocyanurate in shallow spaces to get more R value per inch than you can with fiberglass.

- Gaps between pieces of insulation or insulation and framing can let large amounts of heat escape, diminishing the overall R value.

- Use expanding foam sealant to fill gaps between sheets of rigid insulation.

- R-19 fiberglass insulation, which is meant for a 2 x 6 wall, will become R-11 insulation if compressed into a 2 x 4 wall. Try not to compress fiberglass insulation too much when you install it.

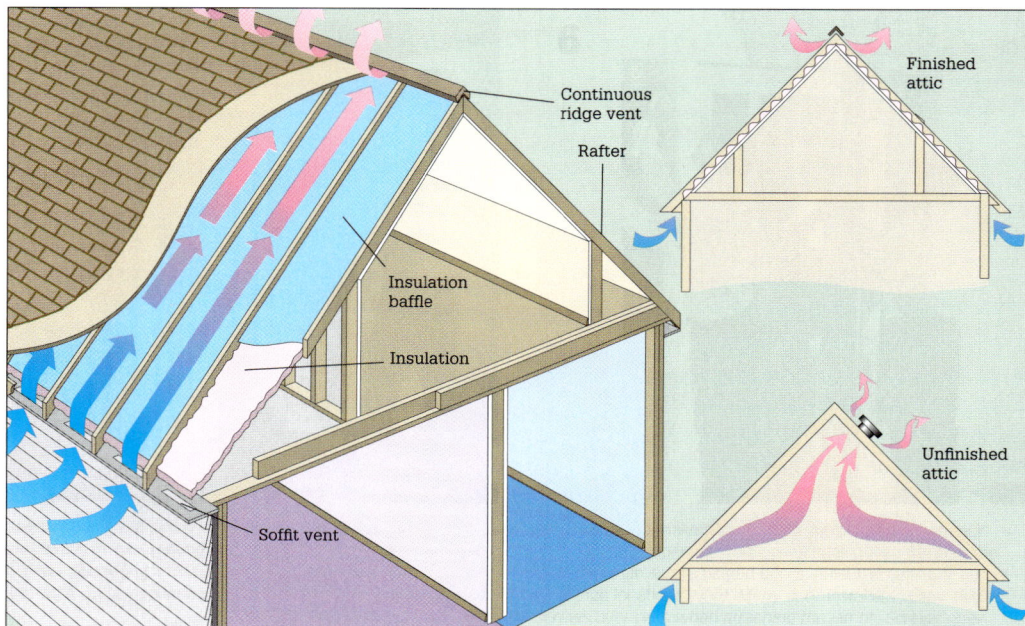

A roof ventilation system works in conjunction with attic insulation: insulation forms a thermal barrier that keeps the home's conditioned air in, while the ventilation system uses outdoor air to keep the roof deck cool and dry. In most unfinished attics, the entire attic space is ventilated, and proper air flow can be achieved with roof vents or gable-wall vents.

Insulating & Ventilating Roofs

Ventilation works in concert with insulation to keep your roof deck healthy. Roofs need ventilation for a number of reasons. During hot weather, direct sunlight can heat a roof considerably, and air flow underneath the roof deck helps lower temperatures, keeping your attic cooler. In cold climates, and particularly in areas with heavy snowfall, roofs need ventilation to prevent ice dams and other moisture problems. As you insulate your attic ceiling, you need to make sure the roof will remain properly ventilated.

Here's how roof ventilation works: air intake vents installed in the soffits—called soffit vents—allow outdoor air to pass under the roof sheathing and flow up toward the ridge, where it exits through one or more exhaust vents. In unfinished attics, with insulation only along the floor, air is allowed to flow from open rafter bays into a common air space under the roof. It can then be exhausted through any of the roof or gable vents. When you finish your attic,

however, you enclose part or all of each rafter bay with insulation and a ceiling finish. A flat attic ceiling will provide some open air space above the ceiling, but air flow still may be limited. With a peaked ceiling, the rafter bays are enclosed up to the ridge, and a single roof vent can serve only one rafter bay. To improve ventilation, install additional roof and soffit vents or a continuous ridge vent, which provides ventilation to all of the rafter bays.

A roof ventilation system must have a clear air path between the intake and exhaust vents. For this reason, most building codes call for one inch of air space between the insulation and the roof sheathing. To ensure this air space remains unobstructed, install insulation baffles in the rafter bays. Also be sure to install enough insulation to meet the recommended R value for your area. This may require increasing the depth of your attic rafters to accommodate the insulation and baffles.

Insulating Roofs ▸

Use insulation baffles to provide a continuous air channel behind the insulation. The baffles should start just in front of the exterior walls' top plates and extend up to the vents. Attach the baffles to the roof sheathing with staples.

Lay fiberglass insulation, stopping short of the baffle opening to avoid restricting air flow. Insulation in the attic floor should cover the exterior walls' top plates but not extend into the soffit cavities.

Increase the rafter depth to make room for thicker insulation by attaching 2 × 2s to the rafter edges. Fasten the 2 × 2s with 3"-long drywall screws. You can also save space by using sprayed-foam insulation.

Options for Ventilating Roofs

Roof vents (box or mushroom type) are commonly used to ventilate unfinished attics. Improve ventilation by adding more roof vents and soffit vents (above, right). If your rafter bays are enclosed all the way to the ridge, be sure the soffit vents and roof vents are installed along the same rafter bays.

Continuous ridge vents are the most effective roof vents, because they ventilate along the entire ridge. It costs less to have one installed during a re-roofing project, but they can be installed onto an existing roof that's in good condition. This type of vent works best when used in conjunction with continuous soffit vents.

Insulating Basements

Insulating basement walls saves energy and increases the comfort level in your basement, but should only be done if the basement walls are dry. Unless water drains away from the house or is controlled by a sump pump, moisture can wick through concrete and block walls and—if trapped by insulation—create serious mold and mildew problems. There are a number of different ways to insulate and frame a basement wall, but no matter how you do it, never put fiberglass insulation directly against a below-grade basement wall. It's acceptable to put a layer of rigid insulation against the wall, followed by fiberglass, but fiberglass in contact with a cold, even slightly damp masonry wall will quickly deteriorate.

Insulating basement walls improves your home's energy-efficiency. Carefully consider the right option for your basement to prevent mold and mildew from forming on moist walls.

What is a Dry Wall? ▸

When building experts warn never to insulate a wall that isn't dry, they have something very specific in mind. A wall that appears dry to the touch may not be classified as dry if it is constantly evaporating small amounts of moisture that will be blocked if you install any kind of vapor retarder (as is likely the case). A dry wall (suitable for interior insulation) is one that is superficially dry to the touch and also meets these criteria:

- Has a positive drainage system capable of removing water that accumulates from any source (this is typically in the form of a sump pump).
- The foundation wall and floor are structured to provide drainage of water away from the house, often through the use of drain tiles and footing drains.

Insulate the rim joist with strips of 2"-thick isocyanurate rigid insulation with foil facing. Be sure the insulation you purchase is rated for interior exposure (exterior products can produce bad vapors). Use adhesive to bond the insulation to the rim joist, and then caulk around all the edges.

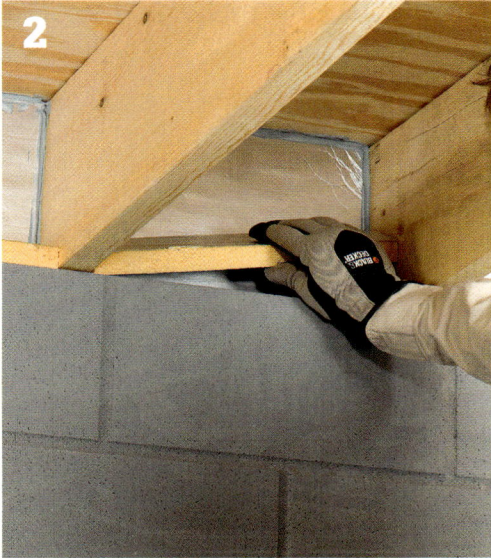

Seal and insulate the top of the foundation wall, if it is exposed, with strips of 1½"-thick, foil-faced isocyanurate insulation. Install the strips using the same type of adhesive and caulk you used for the rim joist insulation.

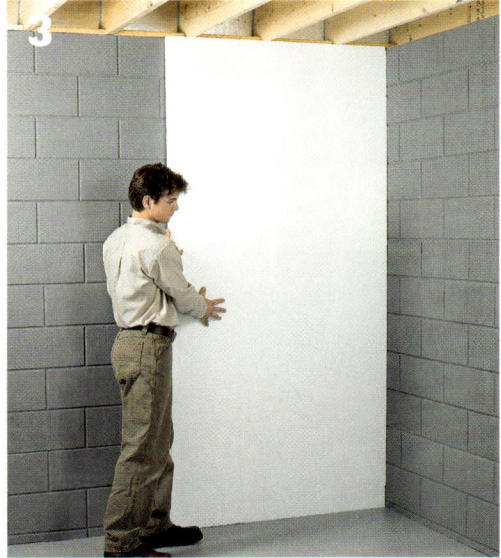

Attach sheets of 2"-thick extruded polystyrene insulation to the wall from the floor to the top of the wall. Make sure to clean the wall thoroughly and let it dry completely before installing the insulation.

Seal the gaps between the insulation boards with insulation vapor barrier tape. Do not caulk gaps between the insulation boards and the floor.

Install a stud wall by fastening the cap plate to the ceiling joists and the sole plate to the floor. If you have space, allow an air channel between the studs and the insulation. Do not install a vapor barrier.

WATER HEATERS

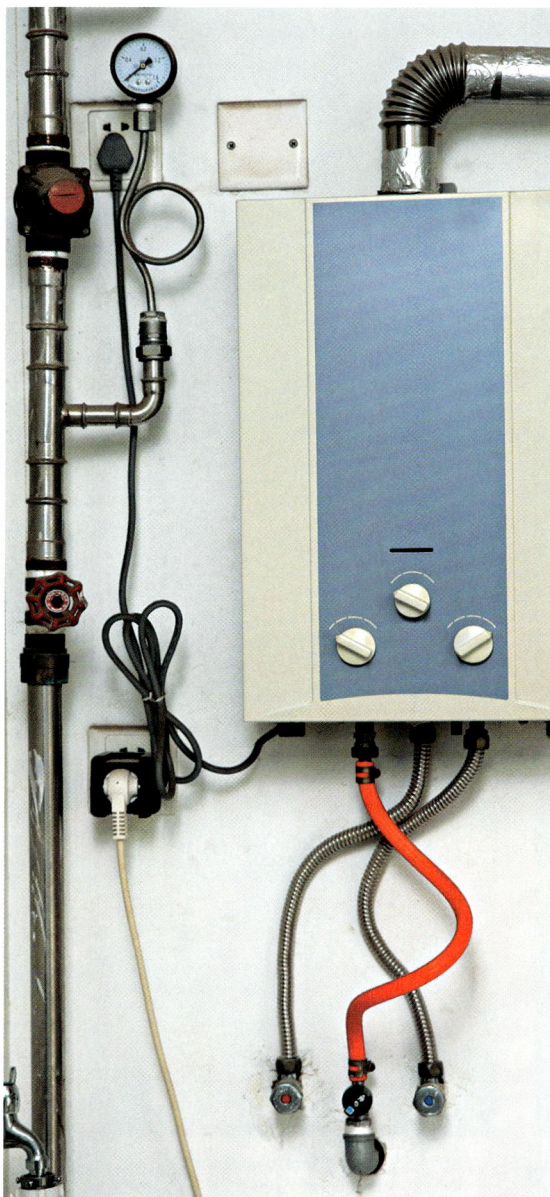

Tankless water heaters heat water as it is needed. Any whole house tankless heater with an Energy Star label qualifies for the tax credit.

In the average household, hot water accounts for roughly 15 cents out of every dollar paid for utility bills, and much of this money is actually spent just keeping the water in the storage tank hot. Conventional hot water heaters are very inexpensive, but their higher utility bills can eat up that initial savings within a few years.

Conventional water heaters are essentially just a large steel tank wrapped with a thin blanket of insulation. Water is warmed by a gas or electric heating element that kicks on whenever the water temperature drops.

High-efficiency water heaters have the same basic design, but use better burners, power venting, and more insulation to achieve lower energy use—generally about seven percent less. Some high-efficiency heaters have received the Energy Star designation, but none of them are efficient enough yet to qualify for the energy-efficiency tax credit.

Gas-condensing water heaters (a new technology coming out in late 2009) also do not yet qualify for the tax credit.

Gas tankless water heaters eliminate the storage tank and instead just heat water as it's needed. The cold water flows into a heat exchanger, where the heat from the gas flame is transferred to the water. Any whole house tankless heater with an Energy Star label qualifies for the tax credit.

Solar hot water heaters store water like conventional water heaters do, but the energy used to warm the water comes from solar collectors. These heaters use a backup heat source for cloudy days. All Energy Star solar heaters qualify for the credit.

Electric heat pump water heaters also qualify for the credit, but are just starting to become available. These work like air source heat pumps, extracting heat from air with a liquid refrigerant and then passing the heated refrigerant through coils in the hot water heater where the heat is transferred to the water.

Qualification

Three types of water heaters currently qualify for the tax credit: whole house tankless heaters, solar water heaters, and electric heat pump water heaters. Products must have an Energy Star designation and a Manufacturer Certification Statement to earn the credit.

Water Heater FAQs ▸

Q – Do any high-efficiency gas storage water heaters qualify for the tax credit?
A – No. Only tankless, solar, and electric heat pump types qualify.

Q – Do small tankless heaters qualify for the credit?
A – No. The minimum approved flow is 2.5 gallons per minute over a 77° rise.

Q – If I install the heater myself, can I add the cost of my labor to the total price for purposes of calculating the credit?
A – No, but check energystar.gov before you fill out your tax return to make sure the rule hasn't changed.

Whole house gas tankless water heaters save an average of $115 a year in utility bills. Residential models heat 4 to 8 gallons a minute—enough to run two or three appliances simultaneously. Tankless heaters start at $1,000 but many utility companies offer rebates that reduce the price. The tax credit is 30% of the product and installation cost, with a maximum credit of $1,500. The credit for a tankless water heater expires in 2010.

Solar water heaters can save over $200 a year. Although initial installation costs can be several thousand dollars or more, the tax credit is 30% of the product and installation cost with no maximum, and doesn't expire until the end of 2016. All Energy Star solar heaters qualify, but the hot water must be used for household use, not swimming pools.

Electric heat pump water heaters can save up to $290 a year. All Energy Star models qualify, and the tax credit is for 30% of the product and installation cost, with a maximum credit of $1,500.

Tankless Water Heaters

Tankless water heaters offer many advantages, including increased energy efficiency and a potentially unending supply of hot water. This is why they have been popular in Europe for a long time and are increasingly common in North America. Fueled by natural gas, or propane, a tankless heater works a bit like an automotive radiator: cold water enters the heater and flows through a matrix of coils, exiting the heater at temperatures from 100 to 140 degree fahrenheit (default temperature on most models is 122 degrees fahrenheit).

A moderate-size tankless water heater will deliver six to eight gallons of heated water per minute—enough volume to supply a shower or bathtub and a sink faucet or two. If your home has multiple bathrooms that are used concurrently, you can install a tankless heater with a higher output rate, such as 10 gallons per minute. But it may also make more sense for you to install multiple water heaters to supply various fixture and appliance "zones" in your home.

Gas-fueled tankless water heaters must be independently vented out of the house with 3-inch stainless steel vent pipe (gas rated). In many cases, you're required to install them in a twin-pipe system, where fresh air is piped directly into a sealed burner from outdoors.

From an efficiency and cost-of-operation standpoint, gas-fueled (either natural gas or liquid propane) burners make a great deal of sense. But installing

A tankless water heater can deliver 6 to 8 gallons of hot water per minute, and is much more energy efficient than a conventional water heater.

one yourself is an extremely challenging and potentially dangerous DIY task, one for a very experienced DIYer or a professional installer. A permit and on-site inspection are required.

Note: The following information is not intended to be comprehensive. Before installing a tankless water heater, the installer should read the installation manual completely and discuss the plan with local plumbing and wiring inspectors.

Save Hot Water ▸

Replace all showerheads and kitchen and bath faucet aerators with low-flow models. It will save thousands of gallons of hot water, as well as reduce total water use.

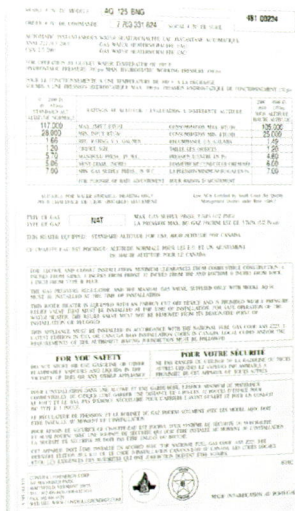

Inspect the rating plate (usually found on the cover of the heater) to make sure that the tankless heater is compatible with your fuel source. Units designed for liquid propane gas cannot be interchanged with units that burn natural gas.

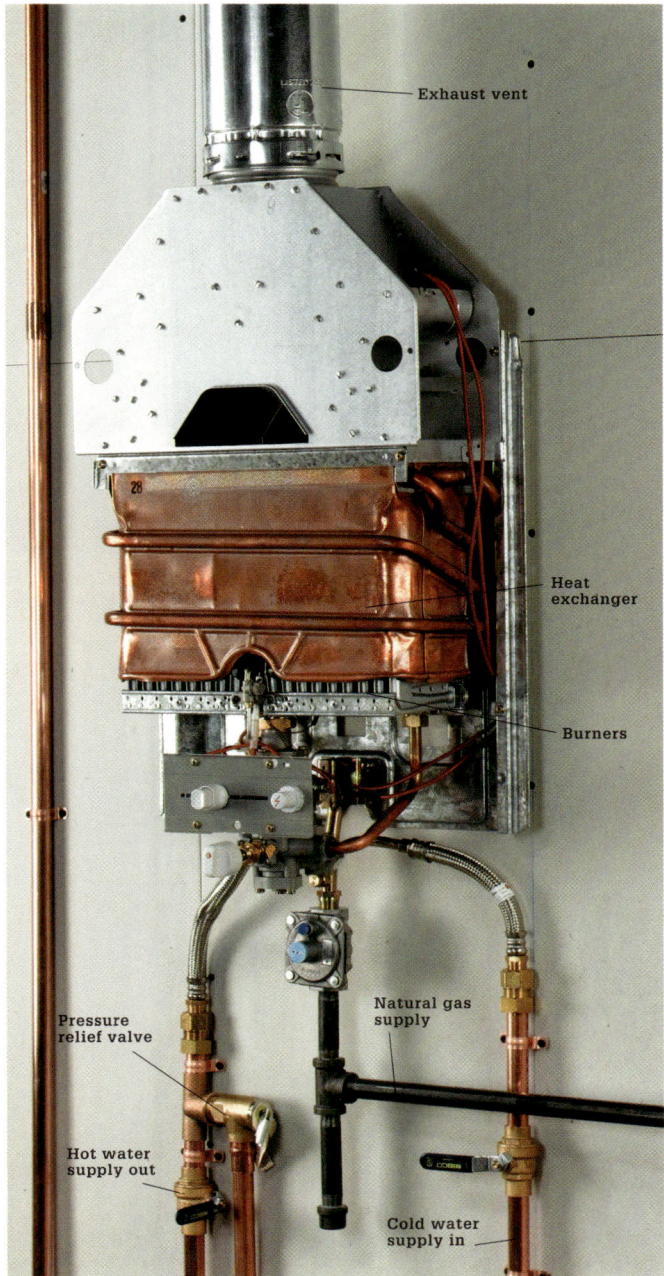

Gas-fueled tankless water heaters are very efficient, but they are also more difficult to install and may require that you replace gas supply pipes from the meter.

How to Install a Tankless Water Heater

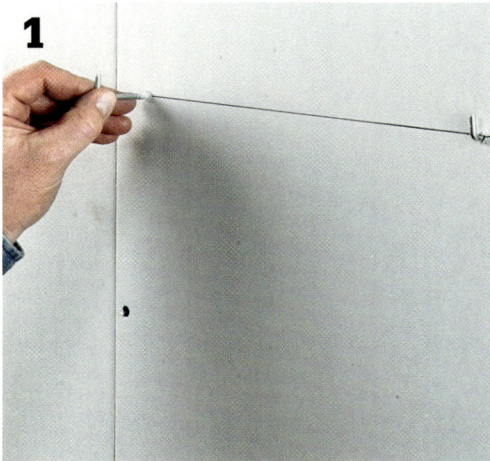

Attach the mounting hardware to the framing members as recommended. Make sure the unit will be level and positioned so the heater unit meets minimum clearance requirements.

Set the heater unit onto the mounting hardware. Run code-approved vent pipe from the unit out of the house. Follow local code regarding length of the vent and placement of the termination.

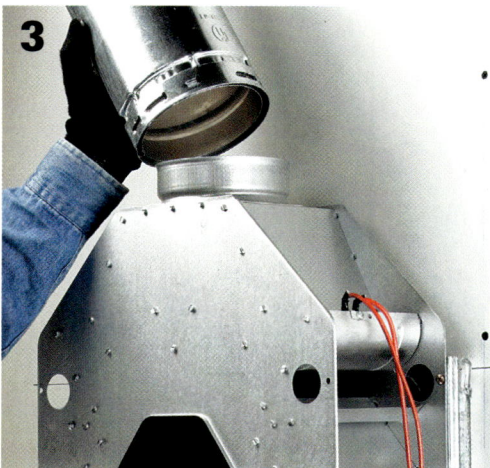

Attach the exhaust connector and gasket at the exhaust vent outlet. Insert the vent pipe into the connector. Install a condensate tube or trap in the exhaust line if required by code.

Run gas supply line from the main and connect to the unit as directed. Be absolutely certain that the pipe material and size meet minimum standards for the unit (flexible copper lines generally are not allowed and black iron pipe is preferred for natural gas). Also make sure the line is equipped with a manual shutoff valve near the heater unit.

Run cold water supply to the water inlet port on the heater unit and connect as directed. Insert an inlet filter screen between the supply line and the inlet port. Make certain that you are hooking the supply to the correct port.

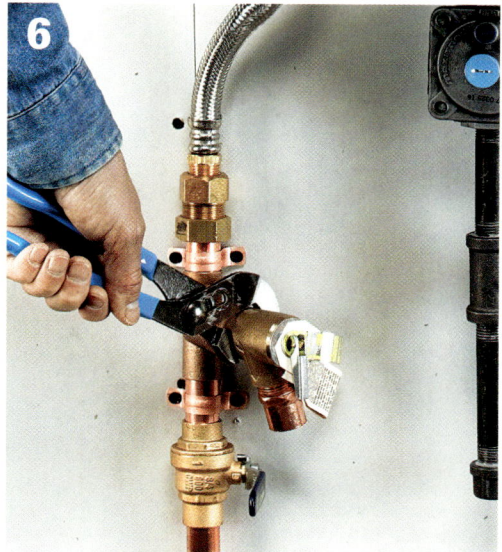

Connect a pressure relief valve (PRV) to the hot supply line, making certain any shutoff valves are downstream from the PRV. Connect the hot water outlet to the correct outlet port with a compression fitting. Attach a discharge line to the PRV if required by code.

Follow manufacturer's instructions to make the electrical connections to operate the blower fan and control panel. Most heater units must be independently grounded, as well. Replace cover plate when finished. Have the tankless water heater inspected before use. This will likely include leak and pressure inspections on the gas and water lines. Replace cover plate when finished

Test the gas line for leaks by brushing soap suds onto the connection. Leaking gas will cause the suds to bubble up. Follow the manufacturer's instructions for setting up, operating, and maintaining your new tankless water heater.

Solar Water Heaters

The science behind solar water heating is quite simple: If you've ever turned on a garden hose that's been left out in the sun (only to get extremely hot water when you expected cold), you pretty much get how it works. In a basic solar hot water system, water or an antifreeze fluid is circulated through rooftop collector units, then down into the house (or swimming pool) where it feeds a system to supply domestic hot water or to supplement space heating equipment.

Solar hot water systems are used in many different climates and are inexpensive and reliable enough to yield relatively quick financial returns in addition to long-term environmental benefits. For most homes, the solar system is used in conjunction with conventional heating equipment, such as a hot water heater or boiler, providing preheated water to the system to reduce its net energy use. On average, solar heaters for domestic hot water are most cost-effective when they supply around 70 percent of a home's hot water. Solar systems supplementing heating equipment are most cost-effective when designed to offset 40 to 80 percent of the home's annual demand.

TYPES OF HOT WATER SYSTEMS

The basic setup of a solar hot water system includes one or more collectors, a storage tank, various control devices, and a network of piping. Indirect systems circulate the same water or fluid through a continuous pipe loop and transfer heat via a heat exchanger. Direct systems run fresh water through the collector's piping and into the home for direct use.

Systems are also defined by their means of circulation: active heaters use an electric pump (which may be solar-powered) to move the water or fluid mechanically. Passive heaters move water without the use of pumps, usually through the natural process of thermosyphoning: as the water in the collector heats up, it rises up into a storage tank while cold water refills the collector tubes.

Solar heaters for domestic hot water may include a separate storage tank that feeds preheated water into a standard tank-style hot water heater or a tankless on-demand heater. The water heater can then boost the temperature of the water for use, as needed. In other systems, solar-heated water is fed directly into a single hot water tank, which typically contains its own conventional heat source.

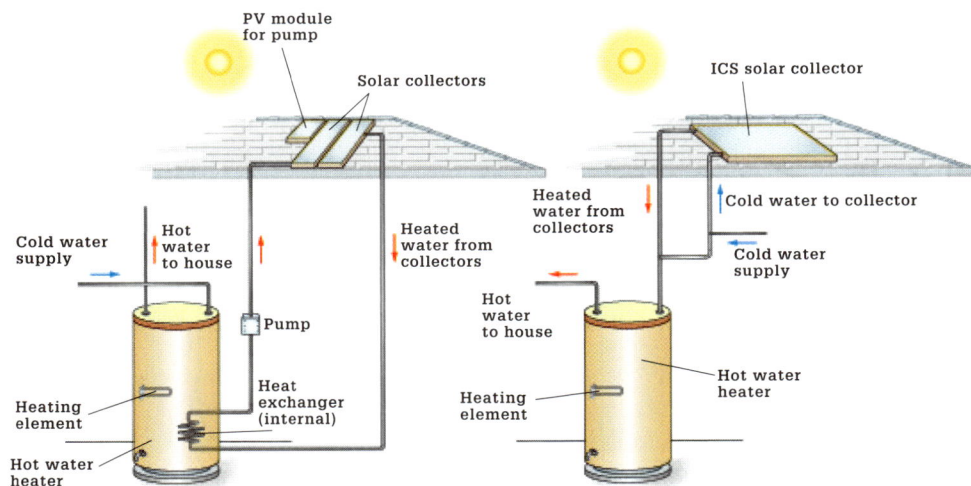

Two systems for domestic hot water: An indirect, active system (left) heats water via a heat exchanger inside a hot water tank and uses a pump to circulate fluid to and from the solar collectors. A direct, passive system (right) heats the same water that gets used in the house and relies on natural processes for circulation.

TYPES OF COLLECTORS

Solar collectors for rooftops and other installations come in a few different varieties. The most widely used type in residential systems is the flat-plate collector, which is essentially a heat-absorbing box filled with winding tubes that carry the water or antifreeze solution for heating. Evacuated tube collectors are made up of parallel rows of glass tubes, each containing a smaller, inner tube that carries the heat transfer fluid. The air space between the inner and outer tubes is vacuumed out (evacuated) to reduce heat loss through convection and conduction. And a third type of collector that's becoming more popular for residential systems is made from plastic polymers (see sidebar, right).

To help consumers and building professionals make informed decisions about solar water systems, there are two groups that provide unbiased performance ratings for different types of solar collectors and hot water systems:

Solar Rating and Certification Corporation

The SRCC is a nonprofit group of solar industry professionals, government energy experts, and consumer advocates. They evaluate and certify solar equipment through their OG-300 program. This group also provides performance estimates for solar products in various climates. Performance ratings and other information are available online at www.solar-rating.org.

Florida Solar Energy Center The FSEC is the Florida state energy research institute. Among its many roles in the solar industry, the FSEC conducts tests to compare the efficiency and economics of flat-plate solar collectors. The institute's website (www.fsec.ucf.edu) includes a list of tested products by manufacturer, plus numerous educational tools for consumers thinking about going solar.

GETTING STARTED WITH SOLAR HOT WATER

Choosing the right system for your home involves many factors, including the local climate, the orientation of your house, your average hot water or heating needs, and the existing systems and how they will integrate with the solar equipment. For help assessing your situation, consult with local solar providers—experienced professionals who design and install the types of systems you're interested in. Local pros know best how to design systems for the prevailing conditions and are up to date on the financial incentives available to local residents.

DIY Solar ▸

Solar water heating has long been available to homeowners wanting to reduce their energy bills, but until recently the systems have never been designed for do-it-yourself installation. One product changing that is the lightweight polymer solar collector. While standard copper or glass tube collectors are housed in heavy rigid panels that must be hoisted onto rooftops with a crane or a small crew, polymer collectors weigh less than ½-lb. per square foot and can easily be installed by two people. They're also flexible and can be rolled up for efficient shipping and transport. Another feature of easy-install solar hot water kits is flexible PEX tubing, which replaces the rigid copper or plastic piping found on standard systems. Flexible tubing is much simpler to install and is easy to route around framing and other obstructions.

The collector shown here can be laid right over standard roofing shingles and mounted with straps and screws. Installation typically takes less than a day.

A wide variety of high-efficiency heating and cooling equipment can qualify for the tax credit—even wood-burning stoves used for supplemental heat.

HEATING & COOLING

Heating and cooling costs account for almost half of household energy use, and energy-efficient systems can reduce those costs significantly. Tax credits can lower the cost of a wide range of high-efficiency heating and cooling systems—even wood-burning stoves. Not all Energy Star products qualify, however, so make sure the product you want to buy has a Manufacturer Certification Statement. The energystar.gov website has links to manufacturers of qualified products, as well as online calculators to help you project savings that may result from installing a new unit.

All eligible heating and cooling systems qualify for a tax credit in 2009 and 2010 equal to 30 percent of the product cost plus installation, up to $1,500—except for geothermal heat pumps, which earn a credit of 30 percent of the total cost with no cap, and can be claimed through 2016. All of these systems generally require professional installation to ensure that they're properly sized for the space and the existing ductwork and have the proper refrigerant charge (for central air and heat pumps).

If you're replacing an old, inefficient heating or cooling unit, you'll notice a big energy savings whether you install a less expensive, mid-efficiency unit or a high-efficiency unit, and the higher efficiency may only gain an extra $100 to $200 savings a year. However, the tax credit and local rebates (if available) can actually make the more efficient unit less expensive.

Note: In order to qualify for the tax credit, both parts of a split system (either central air or heat pump) must be replaced.

FAQs ▶

Q – Do room air conditioners qualify?
A – No, but ductless air conditioners or ductless air source pumps qualify, as long as they meet the criteria for central, ducted systems.

Q – Can I get the credit for both a furnace and a heat pump?
A – Yes, but the total tax credit can't exceed $1,500 unless you're installing a geothermal heat pump.

Q – I heat my house with electric baseboard heat, but I'd like to install a wood-burning stove because I like the way they look. Can I still qualify for the credit?
A – As long as the stove has a thermal efficiency of at least 75% and a Manufacturer Certification Statement and it is placed in service in 2009 or 2010.

Qualification

Central air conditioning units, including ductless systems, require an Energy Efficiency Ratio (EER) of 13 or more and a Seasonal Energy Efficiency Ratio (SEER) of at least 16 if they're split systems. Package systems, where the entire system is outside on the roof or in the yard, require an EER of 12 and a SEER of 14.

Gas or propane forced-air furnaces need an Annual Fuel Utilization Efficiency (AFUE) of at least 95% to qualify for the tax credit. These units are expensive, but the tax credit makes the final price equivalent to a lower efficiency unit. Oil forced-air furnaces require an AFUE of 90% or more.

Package-unit heat pumps are self-contained heating and cooling appliances that are very simple to install. Eligibility requirements for this type of heat pump are HSPF of 8, EER of 12, and SEER of 14.

Air-source heat pumps (split systems) resemble AC units, but they can provide heat to the house in addition to cooling. They require a Heating Seasonal Performance Factor (HSPF) of 8.5, an EER of 12.5, and a SEER of 15.

Quick Fix Tips ▸

Change your air filter every month all year round. A clogged filter reduces furnace efficiency and can cause maintenance problems.

Use a programmable thermostat to control your heating and cooling system. It can pay for itself within months. And remember to change the backup batteries every year.

Biomass stoves can burn wood, wood pellets, corn, plants and other renewable materials. They're available as freestanding stoves, fireplace inserts, or furnaces and qualify for the tax credit if they have a thermal efficiency of at least 75%.

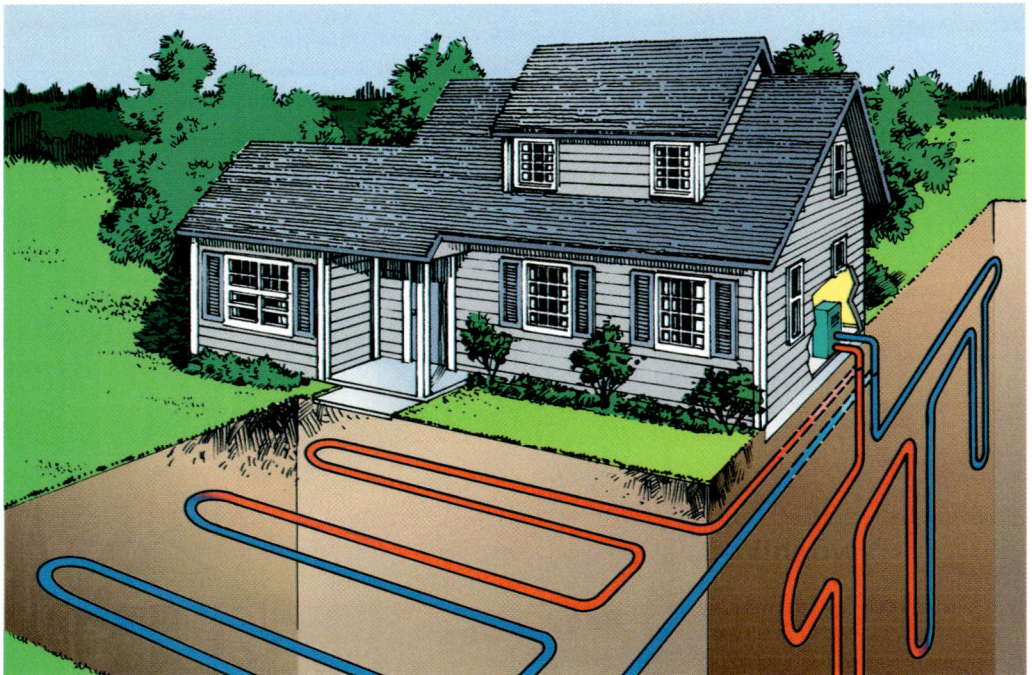

Geothermal heat pumps use the constant temperature of the earth for heating, air conditioning, and hot water. Tubes carrying coolant are buried in the earth either horizontally or vertically, and as the coolant circulates heat is exchanged—either extracted from the ground in winter or dissipated into the ground in summer. All Energy Star heat pumps qualify for the tax credit—30% of the product and installation cost, with no cap, which reduces the high initial cost considerably. Tax credits for geothermal heat pumps are available through 2016, and can be spread over more than one year.

Sealing & Insulating Ductwork

Often some of the biggest heat losses in forced-air systems are through duct joints and the walls of ductwork in unheated parts of the home. Poorly sealed and unsealed joints can allow 15 to 20 percent of the heated supply air to leak into spaces where the heat can't be used, and they contribute to dust buildup in the duct network.

If you live in an older home, chances are the metal ductwork was not sealed, causing significant leakage at joints where straight duct runs meet bends, register boots, and other fittings. In the old days, HVAC contractors may have used standard duct tape to seal joints. This all-purpose tape that's great for quick fixes throughout the house is unsuitable for ductwork—it dries out and can begin to fall off after just a few years. These days, the standard for sealing is duct mastic: a flexible, water-based adhesive that gets into the cracks of joints to create a complete air seal. You can apply duct mastic yourself following the manufacturer's directions.

Ducts can also be sealed with UL-181 certified duct tape, which won't dry and flake off like standard duct tape, but it's generally less effective than mastic.

Another option is to have an HVAC professional blow a latex aerosol into the ductwork, which seals gaps from the inside. For more information, visit www.aeroseal.com.

Most ducts in a forced-air system are made with thin metal that moves air efficiently but is highly heat-conductive. As heated air passes through supply (hot-air) ducts, 10 to 30 percent of the heat can be lost through conduction, and the losses are greatest where ducts run through unheated basements, crawlspaces, and attics. Newer homes often have insulated supply ducts, while older homes often do not.

A simple solution for reducing this heat loss is to wrap the outsides of all supply ducts with an approved insulation and seal the seams with tape. In cold climates, insulation of R-5 to R-8 is recommended. You can use foil-faced batt insulation (with the foil facing out) or use rigid insulation board, sealing the seams on either type with UL-181 duct tape. There are also vinyl-faced products made just for ductwork, which should be sealed following the manufacturer's recommendations.

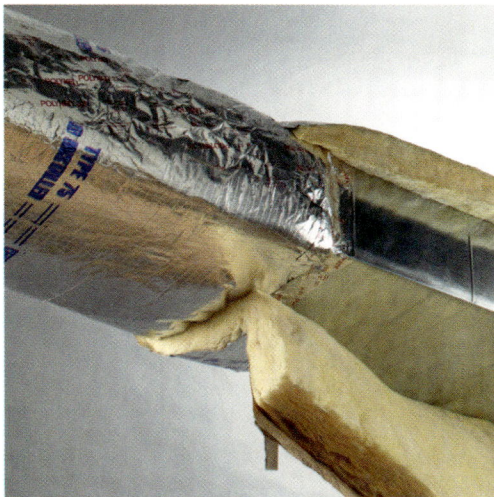

Stop air leakage in duct joints by sealing them with a water-based duct mastic. This is much more effective and long-lasting than standard duct tape.

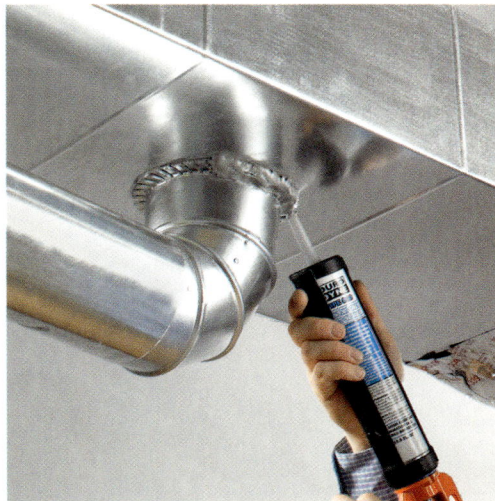

Insulating ductwork in cold spaces stops heat from escaping through the walls of the ducts.

Made with lightweight materials and highly durable materials, today's low-profile solar panels are ideal for discreet rooftop installation.

GENERATING ELECTRICITY

With annual utility bills for single family houses averaging $2,200 a year, the idea of free, renewable energy is increasingly attractive. Unfortunately, the high initial costs for systems large enough to provide all the power for a single family house—usually tens of thousands of dollars—have been an insurmountable barrier for most homeowners. The purpose of the energy-efficiency tax credit is to lower that initial barrier and make these large investments more affordable.

The tax credits for energy generating projects are different than the credits for energy saving projects, and can be taken even if you've already reached the $1,500 maximum credit for energy saving projects. Energy generating projects—which include solar panels, small wind energy systems, fuel cells, solar water heaters, and geothermal heat pumps—earn tax credits for 30 percent of the entire cost of products and labor, including sales tax and site preparation, with no limit except that you can't claim more in credits than you paid in taxes. Energy generating tax credits can be used anytime from 2009 through 2016 and can be carried over from year to year if you have more tax credits than you can use in one year. You can also receive tax credits for energy generating projects at second homes, rental property, and new construction in addition to existing houses–and you can do multiple projects at different houses and receive tax credits for all of them as long as they meet Energy Star guidelines and have a Manufacturer Certification.

Tax credits for 2008 ▶

Tax credits for geothermal heat pumps, solar water heaters, solar panels, small wind energy systems, and fuel cells were available in 2008, but for smaller amounts than in 2009. Unfortunately the new credits are not retroactive, but any unused tax credits from 2008 can be carried forward to 2009 or later.

Solar Panels

Residential photo voltaic (PV) systems supply electricity directly to a home through solar panels mounted on the roof or elsewhere. A solar panel is made up of small solar cells, each containing a thin slice of a silicon, the same stuff used widely in the computer industry. Silicon is an abundant natural resource extracted from the earth's crust. It has semi-conductive properties, so that when light strikes the positive side of the slice, electrons try to move to the negative side. By connecting the two sides with a wire, you create an electrical circuit and a means for harnessing this electrical activity.

Solar cells are grouped together and connected by wires to create a module, or panel. Modules can be installed in a series to create a solar "array." The size of an array, as well as the quality of the semiconductor material, determines its power output.

The electricity produced by solar cells is direct current (DC), which is what most batteries produce and what battery-powered devices run on. Most household appliances and light fixtures run on alternating current (AC) electricity. Therefore, PV systems include an inverter that converts the DC power from the panels to AC power for use in the home. It's all the same to your appliances, and they run just as well on solar-generated power as on standard utility power.

GRID-CONNECTED & OFF-THE-GRID SYSTEMS

Home PV systems can be designed to connect to the local utility network (the power grid) or to supply the home with all of its electricity without grid support. There are advantages and disadvantages to each configuration.

In a grid-connected setup, the utility system serves as a backup to supply power when household demand exceeds the solar system's capacity or during the hours when the sun is down. This obviates the need for batteries or a generator for backup and makes grid-connected systems simpler and less expensive than off-the-grid systems. One of the best advantages of grid connection is that when the solar system's output exceeds the house's demand, it delivers power back to the grid and you may get credit for every watt produced. This is called net-metering and is guaranteed by law in many states; however, not every state requires utility companies to offer it, and not all

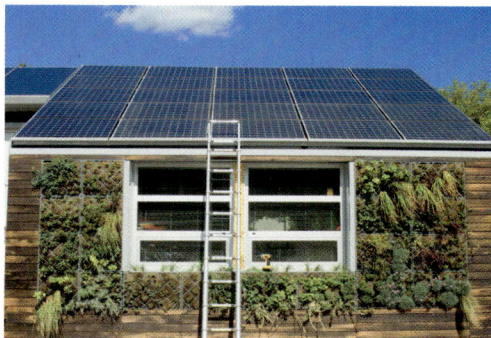

Being off the grid means no electric bill, no concerns about rate hikes, and no utility-based power outages.

Solar cells are building blocks for a future of clean energy.

As green home products move from niche markets into the mainstream, devices such as this electronic energy-monitoring device are becoming easier to locate and more affordable.

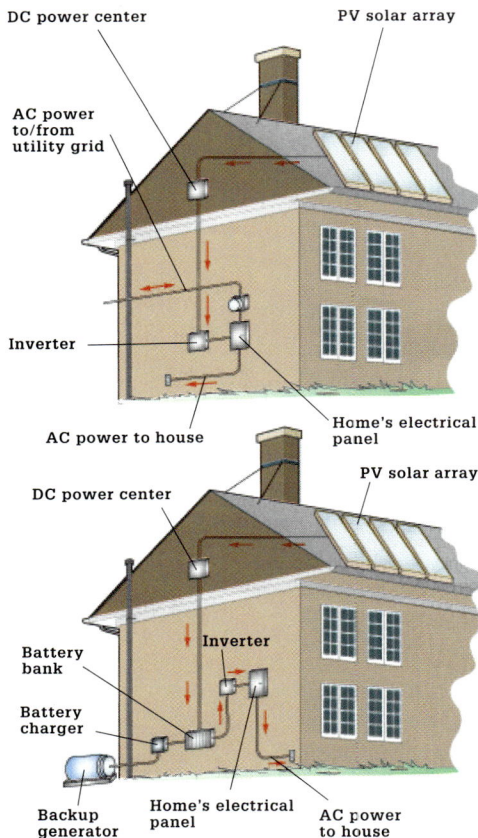

Labels on top diagram:
- DC power center
- PV solar array
- AC power to/from utility grid
- Inverter
- AC power to house
- Home's electrical panel

Labels on bottom diagram:
- PV solar array
- DC power center
- Inverter
- Battery bank
- Battery charger
- Backup generator
- Home's electrical panel
- AC power to house

Grid-connected systems (top) rely on the utility company for supplemental and backup energy. Off-the-grid systems (bottom) are self-sufficient and must use batteries for energy storage and a generator (usually gas-powered) for backup supply.

Off-the-grid, or stand-alone, systems serve as the sole supply of electricity for a home. They include a large enough panel array to meet the average daily demand of the household. During the day, excess power is stored in a bank of batteries for use when the sun is down or when extended cloud cover results in low output. Most stand-alone systems also have a gas-powered generator as a separate, emergency backup.

For anyone building a new home in an undeveloped area, installing a complete solar system to provide your own power can be less expensive than having the utility company run a line out to the house (beyond a quarter-mile or so, new lines can be very costly). There are some maintenance costs, namely in battery replacement, but it's possible to save a lot of money in the long run.

As mentioned, off-the-grid systems are a little more complicated than grid-tied setups. There are the batteries to care for, and power levels have to be monitored to prevent excessive battery run-down and to know when generator backup is required. To minimize power demands, off-the-grid homes tend to be highly energy-efficient. Using super-efficient appliances and taking smaller steps like connecting electronics to power strips that can be switched off to prevent small but cumulative energy losses from devices running in "standby" mode enables homeowners to get by with smaller, less expensive solar arrays.

SOLAR PANEL PRODUCTS

PV modules come in a range of types for different applications and power needs. The workhorse of the group is the glass- or plastic-covered rigid panel that can be mounted to the roof of a house or other structure, on an exterior wall, or on the ground at various distances from the house. Panel arrays can also be mounted onto solar-powered tracking systems that follow the sun for increased productivity.

Rigid modules, sometimes called framed modules, are designed to withstand all types of weather, including hail, snow, and extreme winds, and manufacturers typically offer warranties of 20 to 25 years. Common module sizes range in width from 2 to 4 feet and in length from 2 to 6 feet. Smaller modules may weigh less than 10 pounds, while large panels may be 30 to 50 pounds each.

In addition to variations in size, shape, wattage rating, and other specifications, standard PV modules can be made with two different types of silicon cells. Single crystalline cells contain a higher grade of silicon

companies offer the same payback. Some simply let the meter roll backwards, essentially giving you full retail value for the power, while others buy back power at the utility's standard production price—much less than what they charge consumers.

The main drawbacks of being tied to the grid are that you may still have to pay service charges for the utility connection even if your net consumption is zero, and you're still vulnerable to power outages at times when you're drawing from the grid. But the convenience of grid backup combined with the lower cost and reduced maintenance of grid-tied systems makes them the most popular choice among homeowners in developed areas.

and offer the best efficiency of sunlight-to-electricity conversion—typically around 10 to 14 percent.

Multicrystalline, or polycrystalline, cells are made with a less exacting and thus cheaper manufacturing process. Solar conversion of these is slightly less than single crystalline, at around 10 percent to 12 percent, but warranties on panels may be comparable. All solar cells degrade slowly over time. Standard single crystalline and multicrystalline cells typically lose 0.25 to 0.5 percent of their conversion efficiency each year.

Installing solar panels over an arbor, pergola, or other overhead structure can create a unique architectural element. Here, panels over an arbor provide shade for a patio space while generating electricity for the house.

Mounting solar arrays on the ground offers greater flexibility in placement when rooftop installation is impractical or prohibited by local building codes or homeowners associations.

AMORPHOUS SOLAR CELLS

Another group of solar products are made with amorphous, or thin-film, technology in which non-crystalline silicon is deposited onto substrates, such as glass or stainless steel. Some substrates are flexible, allowing for a range of versatile products, including self-adhesive strips that can be rolled out and adhered to metal roofing and thin solar modules that install just like traditional roof shingles. Amorphous modules typically offer lower efficiency—around five to seven percent—and a somewhat faster degradation of one percent or more per year.

THE ECONOMICS OF GOING SOLAR

While the environmental benefits of solar electricity are obvious and irrefutable, most people looking into adding a new solar system need to examine the personal financial implications of doing so. PV systems cost only a small fraction of what they did 30 years ago, but they're still quite expensive. For example, a three-kilowatt system capable of supplying most or all

This fiber-cement shingle roof features an integrated array of shingles laminated with thin-film PV modules.

of the electricity for a typical green home can easily cost $30,000 (before rebates and credits) and take ten to twenty years to pay for itself even with the tax credit. An off-the-grid system will cost even more. Nevertheless, depending on the many factors at play, going solar can be a sound investment. Think of it as paying for a couple of decades' worth of electricity bills in advance.

Thanks to the long warranties offered by manufacturers and the reliability of today's systems, the costs of maintenance on solar systems are predictably low. This means that most of your total expense goes toward the initial setup of the system. If you divide the setup cost (after rebates and credits) by the number of kilowatt hours (kWh) the system will produce over its estimated lifetime, you'll come up with a per-kWh price that you can compare against your current utility rate. Keep in mind that your solar rate is locked in, while utility rates are almost certain to rise over the lifetime of your system.

Here are some of the factors that tend to affect the cost of a PV system, its effectiveness or efficiency, and the homeowner's return on investment:

- The house and geographic location—how much sun reaches the house; the roof's slope and roofing material
- Electric utility rates and net-metering rates
- Increased home value—PV systems and other energy-saving upgrades can increase a home's resale value (often without raising the property value used for tax assessment)
- Loan rate, if the system is financed

With so many factors to consider, getting to the bottom line can be complicated. Full-service solar companies will perform a cost/benefit analysis to help potential customers make a decision based on the financial picture.

WORKING WITH SOLAR PROFESSIONALS

Companies that provide solar equipment and system design, installation, and maintenance services are rising in number every year. The reputation and reliability of your local solar provider are important considerations, but perhaps more important is the stability of the original equipment manufacturers (OEMs) who produce the main parts of your system and who carry those long warranties. Many of these are large, well-established companies with expertise in energy and/or electronics, so it's a good bet they'll be around in 20 or 25 years to honor their product warranties. Always discuss warranties carefully with your solar provider.

At present, the solar industry really isn't set up for do-it-yourself system design and installation. Professional installation may run you around 15 percent of the total system cost—but remember, 30 percent of that can be take as a tax credit.

Services likely to be included in a provider's system package are:

- Complete system design and installation
- Guarantees on workmanship/installation
- Obtaining building/electrical permits
- Coordinating hookup with utility company
- Obtaining rebates and credits
- Help with OEM warranty claims
- Lifetime technical support

Another thing to be aware of when comparing various providers' quotes, and in talking to other customers, is the actual output of a panel or array as opposed to its STC (or "name plate") wattage rating. Industry sources say the actual useable power of a system is typically about 75 percent of the rated power. This means that if your home needs three kilowatts of power, your system should be rated for four kilowatts.

Kilo-whats? ▸

Confused about kWh's, watts, and amps? Just remember:

Watts is how much power the device needs to operate.
1 kilowatt equals 1000 watts.
Kilowatt-hour (or kWh) measures how long the device was used.

If you leave a 100-watt light bulb on for one hour, you've used 0.10 kWh. If you leave it on for 10 hours, you've used 1 kWh, for which your electrical company will charge you (on average) 11 cents. If you use 1000 kWh in a month your bill will be $110.

Amps times volts equal watts, so if an appliance requires 10 amps of 120 volt household current, it's using 1200 watts – or 1.2 kW. Use it for an hour and you've used 1.2 kWh.

Small Wind Energy Systems

Small wind energy systems can generate power in any weather and at any time of day and are becoming a more common sight in rural and even suburban areas as they shrink in size and price. Small, reasonably quiet systems with towers as low as 30 feet are now available—low enough to comply with most zoning ordinances and slender enough to not be eyesores. Although a small system in an area of moderate wind probably won't generate all the power needed for an average, power-hungry house, they can reduce utility costs enough to pay for themselves in ten or fifteen years.

Wind energy only works if you have a reasonable amount of wind. If the average annual speed in your area is less than 10 mph, wind power may not be a good investment. Before buying anything, research local wind speeds. You can get a rough idea using a wind map of your state, but to get a more exact picture of your location you may need to consult with a manufacturer or dealer, or purchase an anemometer to measure it yourself (this can be expensive). Remember also that a wind energy system needs plenty of open space—generally, turbine blades should be at least 20 feet above any obstacle within 300 feet—and the higher the blades are the more power you'll generate because the wind is stronger and steadier at higher altitudes.

To qualify for the tax credit, the system must have a maximum capacity of no more than 100 kW, which is more than enough power for a large residence. There is no minimum capacity, but systems smaller than 500 watts are meant for low-power applications like sailboats. Wind systems can either be connected to the electrical grid, so that power flows to or from the grid depending on the wind, or hooked up to storage batteries, which then provide backup power when the wind dies.

Prices for systems large enough to make an impact on the average electric bill range from under $10,000 (including installation) to over $50,000, but the 30 percent tax credit and state and local utility rebates can reduce that price substantially.

The Power of Wind & Sun ▸

Wind energy can be combined with solar panels to create a more reliable source of renewable energy.

Wind energy can supply substantial amounts of free energy whenever the wind blows. Prices for systems capable of supplying some or all of an average home's energy needs are dropping rapidly.

Fuel Cells ▸

Fuel cells are an exciting new technology that use hydrogen (the most abundant gas on earth) and oxygen from the air to create electricity, heat, and water—with almost no polluting byproducts. Hydrogen, which has three times as much energy content as gasoline, can be produced from natural gas, crop waste, coal, or other fuel sources, but it can also be produced from water and electricity through electrolysis. Fuel cells are being developed to power everything from cell phones to cars to factories, and are now manufactured for a variety of commercial applications, but the technology is still young and relatively expensive. Only a few companies are selling fuel cells for homes. It is hoped that the tax credits will create more demand for this technology and eventually bring the price down.

Since hydrogen can be created by an electrolyzer, solar panels or wind energy systems can be used as a power source to create it. This means that excess power generated by solar panels on sunny days can be converted into hydrogen fuel and stored in tanks for later use as power for a fuel cell, eliminating the need for bulky, inefficient storage batteries. Demonstration projects have been built showing that this is practical, but consumer versions are not yet available.

Fuel cells qualify for tax credits until 2016, however, and fuel cells may become more readily available by then. To qualify for the credit, fuel cells must be at least 30 percent efficient and have a minimum generating capacity of

0.5 kW. The tax credit is for 30 percent of the cost, but is limited to $500 per 0.5 kW of power capacity and only covers fuel cells used in a primary residence. Many states and utility companies also offer incentives that can further reduce the cost.

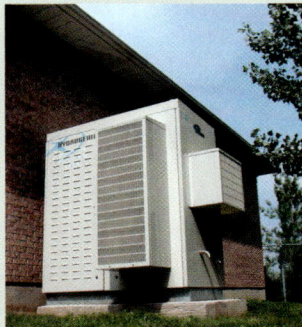

Hydrogen-based fuel cells do not currently have significant residential applications, but because the fuel-cell related aspects of the tax credit program do not sunset until 2016, you may yet be able to take advantage of 30% refunds for hydrogen-fueled home generators for primary and back-up power.

Generating Energy FAQs ▸

Q – Do I need a building permit to install solar panels on my roof?
A – Yes. Any major construction, plumbing, wiring, or mechanical work requires a building permit. It may cost a few dollars extra, but it's a good way to make sure you did everything right.

Q – Can I mount a wind energy system to my roof?
A – Usually not, unless it's a very small one. Contact the manufacturer for more information.

Q – How big a lot do I need for a wind energy system?
A – You'll probably need at least an acre. Any obstacles like trees or buildings block wind and create turbulence, which reduces the amount of available wind energy.

Q – Do utility companies pay the retail price for excess electricity I create?
A – Some of them do. Others pay a wholesale rate. Check with your utility company.

Resources

Aerostar Wind Turbines
www.aerostarwind.com

Alliance to Save Energy
www.ase.org

Bosch (Tankless water heaters)
www.boschhotwater.com

Clear Edge Power (Fuel cells)
www.clearedgepower.com

Database of State Incentives for Renewables
& Efficiency
www.dsireusa.org

Efficient Windows Collaborative
www.efficientwindows.org

Fafco Solar Hot Water Heaters
www.fafco.com

General Electric (Electric heat pump water
heater)
www.ge.com

Home Energy Saver (Online energy audit tool)
hes.lbl.gov

Lennox Hearth Products (Fireplaces)
www.lennoxhearthproducts.com

Mariah Power (Wind energy)
www.mariahpower.com

National Fenestration Rating Council
www.nfrc.org

National Renewable Energy Laboratory (NREL)
www.nrel.gov

Noritz (Tankless water heaters)
www.noritz.com

Online Fuel Cell Information Resource
www.fuelcells.org

Regency Fireplace Products
www.regency-fire.com

Skystream (Wind energy)
www.skystreamenergy.com

The Tax Incentives Assistance Project
www.energytaxincentives.org

United States Green Building Council
www.usgbc.org

U.S. Department of Energy
www.eere.energy.gov

EERE Wind Powering America
www.windpoweringamerica.gov

Energy Star
www.energystar.gov

Recovery Act Clearinghouse
888.363.7289
https://recoveryclearinghouse.energy.gov

U.S. Environmental Protection Agency
www.epa.gov
www.energy.gov/recovery

Wind and Hydropower Technologies
www.windpoweringamerica.gov

Photography Credits

p. 6 (logo) American Recover & Reinvestment Act (ARRA) & Tiger

p. 7 Source: US EPA, courtesy of Energy Star Residential Programs

p. 10 (top) Marvin

p. 11 The Energy Conservatory (www.energyconservatory.com)

p. 16 Jeld-wen

p. 17 (top) New England Metal Roofing, (lower) Clopay

p. 26 Marvin

p. 30 (inset) iStock Photo

p. 48 Clopay

p. 49 (middle row, middle image) GAF Materials Corp., (lower)
iStock Photo

p. 63 Courtesy of NREL/see DOE website at www.energystar.gov
(insulation table)

p. 64 (lower right) Central Fiber Corp. (www.centralfiber.com)

p. 69 (lower right) Alside

p. 72 iStock Photo

p. 73 (top) GE, (lower left) Dawn Solar water heating systems,
(lower right) GE

p. 79 Hot2O (www.fafco.com)

p. 80 Lennox Hearth Products (The Country Collection Bella™ pellet
stove)/www.lennoxhearthproducts.com/800.953.6669

p. 81 (top left) Amana, (top right) Haffner's, (lower left) Lennox,
(lower right) Lennox

p. 82 (top) iStock Photo

p. 84 iStock Photo

p. 85 (top) iStock Photo, (lower) Atlantis Energy sun slates
(www.atlantispv.com)

p. 87 (top left and lower) Namasté Solar / Atlantis Energy
(www.namestesolar.com), (top right) Atlantis Energy sun slates
(www.atlantispv.com)

p. 89 Aerostar

p. 91 FuelCell.org

State Energy Resources for Homeowners

ALABAMA
Energy Division
Department of Economic and Community
    Affairs
401 Adams Avenue
P.O. Box 5690
Montgomery, AL 36103-5690

Phone: 334.242.5290
Fax: 334.242.0552
Website: www.adeca.alabama.gov/Energy/

ALASKA
Alaska Energy Authority
Alaska Industrial Development and Export
    Authority
813 W. Northern Lights Boulevard
Anchorage, AK 99503

Phone: 907.771.3000
Fax: 907.771.3044
Website: www.akenergyauthority.org

ARIZONA
Energy Office
Arizona Department of Commerce
1700 West Washington, Suite 220
Phoenix, AZ 85007

Phone: 602.771.1201
Fax: 602.771.1203
Website: www.azcommerce.com/Energy/

ARKANSAS
Arkansas Energy Office
Arkansas Department of Economic
    Development
One Capitol Mall
Suite 4B-215
Little Rock, AR 72201

Phone: 501.682.1370
Fax: 501.682.270
Website: www.arkansasedc.com/business_
    development/energy/

CALIFORNIA
California Energy Commission
1516 Ninth Street, MS #39
Sacramento, CA 95814-5512

Phone: 916.654.5403
Fax: 916.654.4423
Website: www.energy.ca.gov

COLORADO
Governor's Energy Office
1580 Logan Street, Suite 100
Denver, CO 80203

Phone: 303.866.2100
Fax: 303.866.2930
Email: geo@state.co.us
Website: www.colorado.gov/energy

CONNECTICUT
Energy & Policy Unit, PDPD
Connecticut Office of Policy and Management
450 Capitol Ave MS#52ENR
Hartford, CT 06134-1441

Phone: 860.418.6416
Fax: 860.418.6495
Website: www.opm.state.ct.us/pdpd2/energy/
    enserv.htm

DELAWARE
Delaware Energy Office
1203 College Park Drive
Suite 101
Dover, DE 19904

Phone: 302.735.3480
Fax: 302.739.1840
Website: www.delaware-energy.com

DISTRICT OF COLUMBIA
D.C. Energy Office
Reeds Center
2000 14th Street N.W. Suite 300
Washington, DC 20009

Phone: 202.673.6700
Fax: 202.673.6725
Website: www.dceo.dc.gov/dceo/site

FLORIDA
Florida Energy and Climate Commission
Executive Office of the Governor
600 South Calhoun Street
Suite 251
Tallahassee, FL 32399-1300

Phone: 850.487.3800
Website: www.floridaenergy.org/energy/

GEORGIA
Division of Energy Resources
Georgia Environmental Facilities Authority
233 Peachtree Street, NE
Harris Tower, Suite 900
Atlanta, GA 30303-1727

Phone: 404.584.1000
Fax: 404.584.1069
Website: www.gefa.org/Index.aspx?page=32

HAWAII
Strategic Industries Division
Department of Business, Economic
    Development and Tourism
235 South Beretania Street, Room 502
P.O. Box 2359
Honolulu, HI 96804

Phone: 808.587.3807
Fax: 808.586.2536
Website: www.hawaii.gov/dbedt/info/energy/

IDAHO
Energy Division
Idaho Department of Water Resources
322 E Front Street
P. O. Box 83720
Boise, ID 83720-0098

Phone: 208.287.4800
Fax: 208.287.6700
Email: energyspecialist@idwr.idaho.gov
Website: http://energy.idaho.gov

ILLINOIS
Energy & Recycling Bureau
Illinois Department of Commerce and
    Economic Opportunity
620 East Adams
Springfield, IL 62701-1615

Phone: 217.785.3416
Fax: 217.785.2618
Website: www.commerce.state.il.us/dceo/
    Bureaus/Energy_Recycling/

INDIANA
Office of Energy and Defense Development
101 W. Ohio Street
Suite 1250
Indianapolis, IN 46204

Phone: 317.232.8939
Fax: 317.232.8995
Website: www.energy.in.gov

IOWA
Iowa Office of Energy Independence
Lucas State Office Building
321 E. 12th Street
Des Moines, IA 50319

Phone: 515.281.0187
Website: www.energy.iowa.gov

KANSAS
Kansas Energy Office
Kansas Corporation Commission
1300 SW Arrowhead, Suite 100
Topeka, KS 66604

Phone: 785.271.3170
Fax: 785.271.3268
Email: public.affairs@kcc.state.ks.us
Website: www.kcc.ks.gov/energy/

KENTUCKY
Kentucky Department for Energy Development
    and Independence
500 Mero Street
12th Floor, Capital Plaza Tower
Frankfort, KY 40601-1957

Phone: 502.564.7192
Fax: 504.564.7484
Email: marie.anthony@ky.gov
Website: www.energy.ky.gov

LOUISIANA
Technology Assessment Division
Department of Natural Resources
P.O. Box 94396
617 North Third Street
Baton Rouge, LA 70804

Phone: 225.342.1399
Fax: 225.342.1397
Email: techasmt@la.gov
Website: http://dnr.louisiana.gov/techasmt

MAINE
State Energy Program
Maine Public Utilities Commission
State House Station No. 18
Augusta, ME 04333-0018

Phone: 207.287.3318
Fax: 207.287.1039
Website: www.maine.gov/recovery

MARYLAND
Maryland Energy Administration
1623 Forest Drive, Suite 300
Annapolis, MD 21403

Phone: 410.260.7655
Fax: 410.974.2250
Email: meainfo@energy.state.md.us
Website: www.energy.state.md.us

MASSACHUSETTS
Department of Energy Resources
Executive Office of Energy & Environmental
   Affairs
100 Cambridge Street, Suite 1020
Boston, MA 02114

Phone: 617-626-7300
Fax: 617.727.0030
Email: DOER.Energy@state.ma.us
Website: www.mass.gov/doer/

MICHIGAN
Energy Office
Michigan Department of Labor & Economic
   Growth
P.O. Box 30221
611 W. Ottawa - 4th Floor
Lansing, MI 48909

Phone: 517.241.6228
Fax: 517.241.6229
Email: erdinfo@michigan.gov
Website: www.michigan.gov/energyoffice

MINNESOTA
State Energy Office
Minnesota Department of Commerce
85 7th Place East, Suite 500
St. Paul, MN 55101

Phone: 651.296.4026
Fax: 651.297.7891
Email: energy.info@state.mn.us
Website: www.energy.mn.gov

MISSISSIPPI
Energy Division
Mississippi Development Authority
P.O. Box 849
510 George Street, Suite 300
Jackson, MS 39205

Phone: 601.359.6600
Fax: 601.359.6642
Email: energydiv@mississippi.org
Website: www.mississippi.org

MISSOURI
Energy Center
Department of Natural Resources
P.O. Box 176
1101 Riverside Drive
Jefferson City, MO 65102-0176

Phone: 573.751.2254
Fax: 573.751.6860
Email: energy@dnr.mo.gov
Website: www.dnr.mo.gov/energy/

MONTANA
Department of Environmental Quality
P.O. Box 200901
1100 North Last Chance Gulch Room 401-H
Helena, MT 59620-0901

Phone: 406.841.5240
Fax: 406.841.5222
Website: www.deq.state.mt.us/energy/

NEBRASKA
Nebraska State Energy Office
P.O. Box 95085
Lincoln, NE 68509-5085

Phone: 402.471.2867
Fax: 402.471.3064
Email: energy@neo.ne.gov
Website: www.neo.ne.gov

NEVADA
Nevada State Office of Energy
101 N Carson Street
Carson City, NV 89701

Phone: 775.687.9706
Fax: 775.687.9714
Email: nvp@energy.nv.gov
Website: energy.state.nv.us

NEW HAMPSHIRE
Office of Energy and Planning
State of New Hampshire
4 Chennell Drive
Concord, NH 03301

Phone: 603.271.2155
Fax: 603.271.2615
Website: www.nh.gov/oep/

NEW JERSEY
New Jersey Board of Public Utilities
44 S Clinton Ave
PO Box 350
Trenton, NJ 08625-0350

Phone: 609.777.3300
Fax: 609.777.3330
Email: energy@bpu.state.nj.us
Website: www.bpu.state.nj.us

NEW MEXICO
Energy Conservation and Management Division
New Mexico Energy, Minerals and Natural
   Resources Department
1220 S. St. Francis Drive
P.O. Box 6429
Santa Fe, NM 87505

Phone: 505.476.3310
Fax: 505.476.3322
Email: emnrd.ecmd@state.nm.us
Website: www.cleanenergynm.org

NEW YORK
New York State Energy Research and
   Development Authority
17 Columbia Circle
Albany, NY 12203

Phone: 518.862.1090
Fax: 518.862.1091
Website: www.nyserda.org

NORTH CAROLINA
State Energy Office
North Carolina Department of Administration
1340 Mail Service Center
Raleigh, NC 27699-1340

Phone: 919.733.2230
Fax: 919.733.2953
Email: energyinfo@ncmail.net
Website: www.energync.net

NORTH DAKOTA
Office of Renewable Energy & Energy Efficiency
North Dakota Department of Commerce
P.O. Box 2057
1600 East Century Avenue, Suite 2
Bismarck, ND 58502-2057

Phone: 701.328.5300
Fax: 701.328.2308
Email: dcs@nd.gov
Website: www.communityservices.nd.gov/
   energy/

OHIO
Ohio Energy Office
Ohio Department of Development
77 South High Street, 26th Floor
P.O. Box 1001
Columbus, OH 43216-1001

Phone: 614.466.9797
Fax: 614.466.1864
Email: pboone@odod.state.oh.us
Website: www.ohioenergyoffice.ohio.gov

OKLAHOMA
Office of Community Development
Oklahoma Department of Commerce
P.O. Box 26980
900 N. Stiles
Oklahoma City, OK 73126-0986

Phone: 405.815.6552
Fax: 405.605.2870
Website: www.okcommerce.gov/index.
   php?option=com-content&task=category&s
   ectionid=4&id=164&itemid=712

OREGON
Oregon Department of Energy
625 Marion Street, NE
Salem, OR 97301-3737

Phone: 503.378.5489
Fax: 503.373.7806
Email: energy.in.internet@state.or.us
Website: www.oregon.gov/ENERGY

PENNSYLVANIA
Pennsylvania Bureau of Energy, Innovations, &
    Technology Deployment
Department of Environmental Protection
PO Box 8772
Harrisburg, PA 17105-8772

Phone: 717.783-0540
Fax: 717.783.2703
Email: eppaenergy@state.pa.us
Website: www.depweb.state.pa.us/energy/
    cwp/view.asp?a=3&q=482723

RHODE ISLAND
Rhode Island Office of Energy Resources
1 Capitol Hill, 2nd Floor
Providence, RI 02908

Phone: 401.574.9100
Fax: 401.574.9125
Website: www.riseo.ri.gov

SOUTH CAROLINA
South Carolina Energy Office
1201 Main Street, Suite 430
Columbia, SC 29201

Phone: 803.737.8030
Fax: 803.737.9846
Website: www.energy.sc.gov

SOUTH DAKOTA
Energy Management Office
Bureau of Administration
523 E. Capitol Avenue
Pierre, SD 57501-3182

Phone: 605.773.3899
Fax: 605.773.5980
Email: BOAGeneralInformation@state.sd.us
Website: www.state.sd.us/boa/ose/OSE_
    Statewide_Energy.htm

TENNESSEE
Energy Policy Section
Department of Economic & Community
    Development
312 8th Avenue North, 10th Floor
Nashville, TN 37243

Phone: 615.741.2994
Fax: 615.741.5070
Website: http://tennessee.gov/ecd/recovery/
    sep.html

TEXAS
State Energy Conservation Office
Texas Comptroller of Public Accounts
111 E. 17th Street
11th Floor
Austin, TX 78701

Phone: 512.463.1931
Fax: 512.475.2569
Website: www.seco.cpa.state.tx.us

UTAH
Utah State Energy Program
Utah Geological Survey
1594 West North Temple, Suite 3110
P.O. Box 146100
Salt Lake City, UT 84114-6100

Phone: 801.537.3300
Fax: 801.538.4795
Email: dbeaudoin@utah.gov
Website: www.geology.utah.gov/sep/

VERMONT
Energy Efficiency Division
Vermont Department of Public Service
112 State Street, Drawer 20
Montpelier, VT 05620-2601

Phone: 802.828.2811
Fax: 802.828.2342
Email: vtdps@psd.state.vt.us
Website: publicservice.vermont.gov/divisions/
    energy-efficiency.html

VIRGINIA
Division of Energy
Virginia Department of Mines, Minerals &
    Energy
202 North Ninth Street, 8th Floor
Richmond, VA 23219

Phone: 804.692.3200
Fax: 804.692.3238
Website: www.dmme.virginia.gov/
    divisionenergy.shtml

WASHINGTON
Washington Energy Policy Office
Washington State Office of Trade and Economic
    Development
P.O. Box 43173
906 Columbia Street S.W.
Olympia, WA 98504-3173

Phone: 360.725.3118
Fax: 360.586.0049
Website: www.commerce.wa.gov

WEST VIRGINIA
Energy Efficiency Office
West Virginia Development Office
State Capitol Complex Building 6, Room 645
1900 Kanawha Boulevard East
Charleston, WV 25305

Phone: 304.558.2234
Fax: 304.558.0362
Website: www.energywv.org/community/eep.
    html

WISCONSIN
Wisconsin Office of Energy Independence
17 West Main Street, #429
Madison, WI 53702

Phone: 608.261.6609
Fax: 608.261.8427
Website: www.energyindependence.wi.gov

WYOMING
Business & Industry Division - State Energy
    Program
Wyoming Business Council
214 West 15th Street
Cheyenne, WY 82002-0240

Phone: 307.777.2800
Fax: 307.777.2837
Email: tfuller@wybusiness.org
Website: www.wyomingbusiness.org/business/
    energy.aspx

Index